LAKE
DIST

CLIMBS AND SCRAMBLES

MOUNTAINEERING DAYS OUT
ON THE LAKELAND FELLS

Design and production by Vertebrate Publishing, Sheffield
www.v-publishing.co.uk

LAKE DISTRICT CLIMBS AND SCRAMBLES

MOUNTAINEERING DAYS OUT
ON THE LAKELAND FELLS

STEPHEN GOODWIN

LAKE DISTRICT CLIMBS AND SCRAMBLES

MOUNTAINEERING DAYS OUT
ON THE LAKELAND FELLS

First published in 2015 by Vertebrate Publishing

ISBN 978-1-910240-02-1

Cover photo: Topping out on *Needle Ridge*, The Napes, with Wasdale Head beyond. Photo: Phil Blanshard. Back cover: Pillar Rock seen from the Ennerdale approach. All photography by Stephen Goodwin, unless otherwise credited.

WARNING

Rock climbing is an activity with a danger of personal injury or death. If you climb the presumption is that you are aware of and accept these risks together with responsibility for your activities and your safety. Climbs change unpredictably; holds fall off, rock becomes dirty, in-situ gear deteriorates or disappears. Even a minor alteration can have a dramatic effect on the difficulty or seriousness of a route. There can be no presumption that any given climb will be found in the condition described. It is therefore essential that climbers judge the seriousness or difficulty of any route before committing themselves.

Every effort has been made to achieve accuracy of information in this guidebook. The author, publisher and copyright owners can take no responsibility for: loss of injury (including fatal) to persons; loss or damage to property or equipment; trespass, irresponsible behaviour or any other mishap that may be suffered as a result of following the route descriptions or advice offered in this guidebook. The inclusion of a track or path as part of a route, or otherwise recommended, in this guidebook does not guarantee that the track or path will remain a Right of Way. If conflict with landowners arises we advise that you act politely and leave by the shortest route available. If the matter needs to be taken further then please take it up with the relevant authority.

Contents

Lorton Gully ascended, the author gazes over the vale of Loweswater from Grasmoor End.

Introduction

Late morning in Mirk Cove. The name doesn't sound too encouraging: a place of mists and rain. But today the reality is different, almost sunny. We've just picked our way down into the cove, tucked away above Ennerdale, and are looking up the east buttress of Steeple – mightily impressed. We hadn't expected to see such a clean sweep of rock right down into the cove.

Photos of *Steeple Buttress* are not abundant; certainly we had not seen one. The route was first climbed back in 1957, but how many times since, we wonder? There are no signs of passage, no worn footholds or time-scarred gear pockets, and though the general line is straightforward, the rock becomes greasy higher up. By the time we reach Steeple's summit cairn, the traditional grading of V Diff seems questionable: fine were this a predictable valley crag, but Mirk Cove is as remote as it gets for the Lake District. No place to mess up.

Nor is Steeple's top nearing the end of our day. There is still the hike over Red Pike and the scramble up the north end of Yewbarrow to come; we will have been on the move for nine hours before we reach the car parked by Wastwater.

And movement, in a sense, is what this little book is all about: movement over moor and rock and felltop in England's mountainous corner – the Lake District. It's a connoisseur's blend of climbing in the easier grades up to Severe, scrambling and plenty of tough hiking. Put all three activities together and you have mountaineering.

The twenty itineraries included here have one essential thing in common: in that classic understatement, each is intended as 'a good day out'. On most you will be carrying a rope, scrambling up to a high crag, climbing an airy ridge or tiered buttress, continuing over a mountain top and finding an interesting route back to the valley.

The Lake District was the birthplace of rock climbing and on many of these routes you will be following in the hand and footholds of the Victorian pioneers. Yet despite such pedigree, on all but the most popular scrambles, notably *Sharp Edge* and *Striding Edge*, you are likely to have the route to yourselves. Coiling the rope at the top of say, The Napes or Steeple, afternoon light over the Irish Sea, and a few more felltop miles to go: there's a quiet satisfaction that I hope this little book can share.

Stephen Goodwin

About the routes

All twenty routes are conceived as full days out during which you will be scrambling, and in most cases, rock climbing on the higher crags, and walking considerable distances over rough ground. A rope is required on sixteen of the twenty routes.

The grades of the climbs range from Moderate to Severe, with most either Difficult or Very Difficult. The scrambles are graded in the conventional system of 1 to 3, with 3 being the hardest. On Grade 3 scrambles it is advisable to at least carry, and probably use, a rope.

Craft and safety

This book is not intended as a teaching manual. While the rock climbs are in the easier grades, on all the routes involving roped climbing at least one member of the party should be experienced at leading up to the grade specified in the route summary and at placing protection. That said, for other members of the party, these classic routes are a great place to learn the climber's craft and hone one's skills.

The **summary** and **route description** should be studied carefully before setting out. The **time** given for each day's expedition is on the generous side. There is some allowance for snack breaks and photo stops, but prolonged lunches should be added in. **Heights** of peaks are as shown on the relevant OS map; estimates of crag heights and the length of climbs and pitches have generally been rounded to the nearest 10 or 5 metres.

Weather, the party's experience and prior knowledge of the route will also affect timings and grades. Most rock climbs become harder when wet, particularly those where holds have become polished. While the climb may still be 'do-able', it is likely to take longer and require the placing of more protection.

Kit

Think carefully about how much kit to carry. The art is in finding a balance between lightness and safety. Experienced climbers will have their own favoured systems. The author found a pair of 50-metre ropes best for most of the rock climbs – the weight can be shared and double-roping enables more pitches to be linked – together with a basic set of nuts (1 to 10), extenders and three slings, plus two or three medium-sized cams for the harder routes.

A helmet is recommended for all the rock climbs and for scrambles where there is a risk of stones being dislodged – definitely the case in the Great End gullies.

Footwear

While most of the traditional routes here were climbed in big boots for decades, in truth rock climbing is more fun in a well-fitting pair of shoes made for the job. The extra weight on the walk-in is worth it. For scrambles though, where rock is likely to be interspersed with grass or scree, keep your boots on.

Another, increasingly popular, alternative is to wear a pair of 'approach' shoes. Essentially a supportive trainer with a decent sole, these are a halfway house between big boots and rock shoes. They offer some of the lightweight dexterity of climbing shoes, but retain the grip, and a little of the support, of boots.

Mobile phones

There is no mobile phone reception over much of the area covered. You are thereby liberated from the phone's tyranny, but are also without its reassurance.

Mountain Rescue

In case of an emergency **dial 999 and ask for Police and then Mountain Rescue**. Where possible give a six-figure grid reference of your location or that of the casualty. If you don't have reception where you are, try and attract the help of others around you. The usual distress signal is six short blasts on a whistle every minute. If you don't have a whistle, then shouting may work.

Mountain Rescue by SMS text

Another option in the UK is contacting the emergency services by SMS text – useful if you have a low battery or intermittent signal, but you do need to register your phone first. To register, simply text 'register' to 999 and then follow the instructions in the reply. Do it now – it could save yours or someone else's life. **www.emergencysms.org.uk**

Access and conservation

All twenty routes are within the Lake District National Park, an area not only of outstanding natural beauty but home to a treasury of upland birds and plants – some of them rare and threatened. While the sight of a peregrine falcon quartering the cliff top is a thrilling and not infrequent occurrence on the crags included here, if you are disturbing the bird during nesting, you are committing an offence and the penalties can be severe.

The elusive ring ouzel – like a blackbird with a white bib – may also be seen on some of these routes, particularly on the western fells. Gullies and ledges, away from the depredations of sheep, harbour flowering herbs, heathers and rare sub-arctic species. The Helvellyn range is the most of important area in England for arctic alpine plants such as saxifrages. Rare plants enjoy similar protection to the birds; so watch where you tread.

The climbs included here are not usually subject to access restrictions during the nesting season (Feb/Mar to end June). Lake District nesting restrictions can be viewed on the BMC and FRCC websites: **www.thebmc.co.uk** **www.frcc.co.uk**

The Countryside Code

Be safe – plan ahead

Even when going out locally, it's best to get the latest information about where and when you can go; for example, your rights to go onto some areas of open land may be restricted while work is carried out, for safety reasons or during breeding and shooting seasons. Follow advice and local signs, and be prepared for the unexpected.

- Refer to up-to-date maps or guidebooks.
- You're responsible for your own safety and for others in your care, so be prepared for changes in weather and other events.
- There are many organisations offering specific advice on equipment and safety, or contact visitor information centres and libraries for a list of outdoor recreation groups.
- Check weather forecasts before you leave, and don't be afraid to turn back.
- Part of the appeal of the countryside is that you can get away from it all. You may not see anyone for hours and there are many places without clear mobile phone signals, so let someone else know where you're going and when you expect to return.

Leave gates and property as you find them

Please respect the working life of the countryside, as our actions can affect people's livelihoods, our heritage, and the safety and welfare of animals and ourselves.

- A farmer will normally leave a gate closed to keep livestock in, but may sometimes leave it open so stock can reach food and water. Leave gates as you find them or follow instructions on signs; if walking in a group, make sure the last person knows how to leave the gates.
- In fields where crops are growing, follow the paths wherever possible.
- Use gates and stiles wherever possible – climbing over walls, hedges and fences can damage them and increase the risk of farm animals escaping.
- Our heritage belongs to all of us – be careful not to disturb ruins and historic sites.
- Leave machinery and livestock alone – don't interfere with animals even if you think they're in distress. Try to alert the farmer instead.

Protect plants and animals, and take your litter home

We have a responsibility to protect our countryside now and for future generations, so make sure you don't harm animals, birds, plants or trees.

- Litter and leftover food doesn't just spoil the beauty of the countryside, it can be dangerous to wildlife and farm animals and can spread disease – so take your litter home with you. Dropping litter and dumping rubbish are criminal offences.
- Discover the beauty of the natural environment and take special care not to damage, destroy or remove features such as rocks, plants and trees. They provide homes and food for wildlife, and add to everybody's enjoyment of the countryside.
- Wild animals and farm animals can behave unpredictably if you get too close, especially if they're with their young – so give them plenty of space.
- Fires can be as devastating to wildlife and habitats as they are to people and property – so be careful not to drop a match or smouldering cigarette at any time of the year. Sometimes, controlled fires are used to manage vegetation, particularly on heaths and moors between October and early April, so please check that a fire is not supervised before calling 999.

Keep dogs under close control

The countryside is a great place to exercise dogs, but it is the owner's duty to make sure their dog is not a danger or nuisance to farm animals, wildlife or other people.

- By law, you must control your dog so that it does not disturb or scare farm animals or wildlife. You must keep your dog on a short lead on most areas of open country and common land between 1 March and 31 July, and at all times near farm animals.
- You do not have to put your dog on a lead on public paths as long as it is under close control. But as a general rule, keep your dog on a lead if you cannot rely on its obedience. By law, farmers are entitled to destroy a dog that injures or worries their animals.
- If a farm animal chases you and your dog, it is safer to let your dog off the lead – don't risk getting hurt by trying to protect it.
- Take particular care that your dog doesn't scare sheep and lambs or wander where it might disturb birds that nest on the ground and other wildlife – eggs and young will soon die without protection from their parents.
- Everyone knows how unpleasant dog mess is and it can cause infections – so always clean up after your dog and get rid of the mess responsibly. Also make sure your dog is wormed regularly.

Consider other people

Showing consideration and respect for other people makes the countryside a pleasant environment for everyone – at home, at work and at leisure.

- Busy traffic on small country roads can be unpleasant and dangerous to local people, visitors and wildlife – so slow down and, where possible, leave your vehicle at home, consider sharing lifts and use alternatives such as public transport or cycling. For public transport information, phone Traveline on **0871 200 2233**.
- Respect the needs of local people – for example, don't block gateways, driveways or other entry points with your vehicle.
- By law, cyclists must give way to walkers and horse riders on bridleways.
- Keep out of the way when farm animals are being gathered or moved and follow directions from the farmer.
- Support the rural economy – for example, buy your supplies from local shops.

Maps, descriptions, distances

While every effort has been made to maintain accuracy within the maps and descriptions in this guide, we have had to process a vast amount of information and we are unable to guarantee that every single detail is correct.

Please exercise caution if a direction appears at odds with the route on the map. If in doubt, a comparison between the route, the description and a quick cross-reference with your map (along with a bit of common sense) should help ensure that you're on the right track.

Note that distances have been measured off the map, and map distances rarely coincide 100% with distances on the ground. Please treat stated distances as a guideline only.

Ordnance Survey maps are the most commonly used, are easy to read and many people are happy using them. If you're not familiar with OS maps and are unsure of what the symbols mean, you can download a free OS 1:25,000 map legend from **www.ordnancesurvey.co.uk**

Here are a few of the symbols and abbreviations we use on the maps and in our directions:

Acknowledgements

The author would like to thank the following for their help:

Most of the routes were explored in the company of stalwarts of the Eden Valley Mountaineering Club, notably Phil Blanshard, Ron Kenyon, Catherine Kenyon, Eric Parker, Al Davis, Steve Prior, Soo Redshaw, Julian Davey and Paul Goulding. Thanks to you all.

My gratitude also to Julian Cooper for companionship and spirited debate on long walk-ins, and similarly to Dave Hellier, Steve Lenartowicz and Clare Humphry. Thanks also to Alex Reid, Jo Campbell, Stephen Venables and Simon Yates.

Last but not least, heartfelt thanks to my wife Lucie, for her presence and support on and off the hill – and forbearance when I'd declare yet one more hike was required to catch the light on some distant crag.

Wast Water and The Screes from Dore Head.

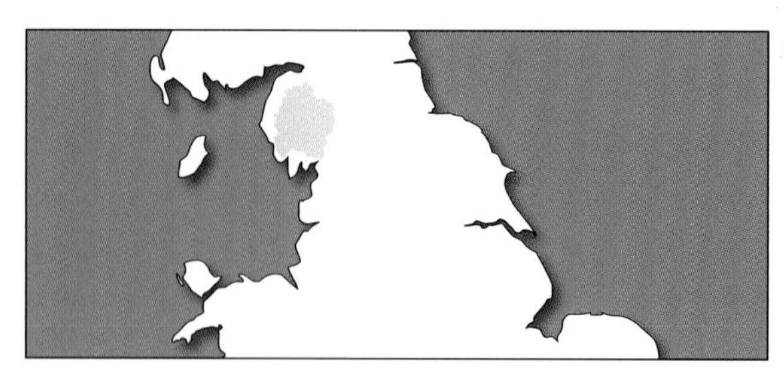

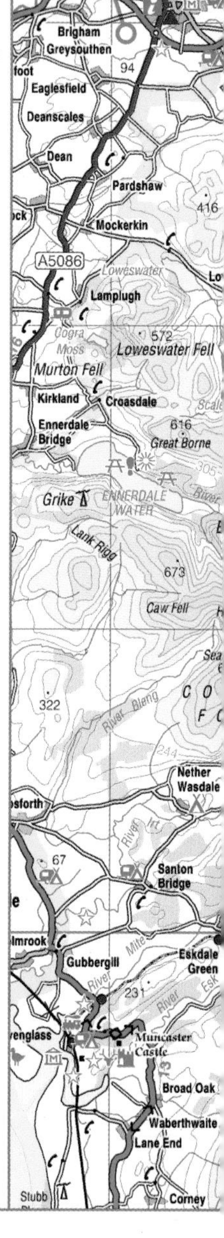

Area Map & Route Finder

Section 1 **Borrowdale & the North-West Lakes**

Section 2 **Langdale & Ullswater**

Section 3 **Dow, Wasdale & the South-West Lakes**

SKIDDAW FOREST
SKIDDAW
Mungrisdale
Berrier
Troutbeck
Saddleback or Blencathra
Scales
Threlkeld
KESWICK
Millbeck
Applethwaite
Thornthwaite
Lorton
Lord's Seat
Whinlatter Pass
Braithwaite
Portinscale
Stair
Grisedale Pike
Grasmoor
Causey Pike
DERWENT WATER
Little Town
Derwent Fells
Newlands Hause
Grange
Buttermere
Buttermere Fell
Rosthwaite
Seatoller
Honister Pass
Seathwaite
Stonethwaite
Borrowdale Fells
High Stile
Scarth Gap Pass
Hay Stacks
Pillar
Black Sail Pass
Kirk Fell
Great Gable
Glaramara
Sty Head
Wasdale Head
Great End
Lingmell
SCAFELL PIKE
SCA FELL
Bow Fell
Stake Pass
High White Stones
Langdale Pikes
Watendlath
High Seat
THIRLMERE
Blea Tarn
Ullscarf
Dunmail Raise
Wythburn Fells
CUMBRIAN MOUNTAINS
LAKE DISTRICT NATIONAL PARK
Stone Circle
Great Dodd
Legburthwaite
Matterdale End
Dowthwaitehead
Dockray
Aira Force
Glenridding
Patterdale
HELVELLYN
Grisedale Tarn
Seat Sandal
Brothers Water
Hartsop
Hayeswater
Kirkstone Pass
Kirkstone Pass Inn
Bridgend
Sandwick
Martindale
Beda Fell
High Street
Hutton
Wreay
Longthwaite
Watermillock
Outward Bound Mountain School
Rydal Fell
Grasmere
Rydal Mount
Rydal Water
Rydal
Chapel Stile
Elterwater
Little Langdale
AMBLESIDE
Clappersgate
Skelwith Bridge
Waterhead
Troutbeck
Town End
Townend
Troutbeck Bridge
WINDERMERE
BOWNESS-ON-WINDERMERE
Wrynose Pass
Hardknott Pass
ROMAN FORT
Cockley Beck
Boot
Eskdale
Harter Fell
Birker Force
Stanley Force
Devoke Water
Seathwaite Tarn
THE OLD MAN OF CONISTON
Coniston
Hawkshead
Outgate
High Wray
Claife Heights
Esthwaite Water
Sawrey
Hill Top
Ferry
Bowmanstead
Brantwood
Torver
GRIZEDALE FOREST
Grizedale
Satterthwaite
Furness Fells
CONISTON WATER
Seathwaite
Hall Dunnerdale
Caw
Stickle Pike
Ulpha
Broughton
Storrs Hotel
Winster
A66
A591
A5091
A592
A593
B5289
B5292
B5322
B5343
B5285
CONTAINS ORDNANCE SURVEY DATA © CROWN COPYRIGHT AND DATABASE RIGHT

1

Borrowdale & the North-West Lakes

With Borrowdale at its heart, the Lake District's north-west provides rich abundance, from the easy – but airy! – scramble along Blencathra's *Sharp Edge* to fine trad' climbing on Grey Crag, overlooking Buttermere. Add in the classic *Needle Ridge* on The Napes, the dark recesses of *Lorton Gully*, plus a whole lot more, and you're spoilt for choice.

On Rosthwaite Cam after an ascent on Doves' Nest (climber Eric Parker).

Cam Crag above Langstrath.

01 **Corvus & Cam Crag Ridge** 12km Diff

A Borrowdale classic climb to the felltops

STONETHWAITE – **BORROWDALE CHURCH** – **THE COMBE** (also known as Combe Gill) – **RAVEN CRAG** (*Corvus*, Diff) – **GLARAMARA** – *Cam Crag Ridge*, Grade 2 – **LANGSTRATH** – **STONETHWAITE**

The day

Corvus, a 160-metre Diff on Raven Crag, high in the valley of The Combe at the south end of Borrowdale, is not only a climb of full value but combines seamlessly with a felltop walk and scrambling descent to give a great all-round day out.

One of the attractions of Raven Crag is that it has the qualities of a high crag without actually standing so high in the mountains that in poor weather it is shrouded in cloud. Not that a bit of wet rules out *Corvus*. It is, as they say, 'a route for all seasons'.

The name *Corvus* (Latin for the crow family) was bestowed by Bentley Beetham, the master from Barnard Castle School whose explorations over more than thirty years yielded many of Borrowdale's classic routes in the easier grades. He climbed *Corvus* solo on 10 June 1950 and, three weeks later, added a harder companion route nearby – *Corax* (Mild Severe).

It is this bird – *Corax*, the raven – that you are most likely to see on the eponymous crag, soaring above the cliff edge or diving in dramatic aerobatics into the combe. As you focus on the next handhold, or gaze from the belay, it's the distinctive one-note tok of the raven that plucks your attention.

The raven likely will be watching as you coil the rope and turn to the steady ascent south over the broad fell to the nobbly summit of Glaramara (783 metres). From here, locating the top of *Cam Crag Ridge* requires attentive felltop navigation. However an emerging scrape in the grass soon lures you to the crest, and there lies Langstrath Beck meandering at your feet – 300 metres below.

Beetham included *Cam Crag Ridge* in his 1953 FRCC guide to Borrowdale as a 'moderate' climb, which is rather overgrading it. Nor does it have the character of a sharp, rocky ridge, more a series of short buttresses and steps set on a steep shoulder of fell. In ascent, sticking to the rocky bits, it is a delight and well worth an outing in its own right. However in descent any unnerving moves can be avoided by keeping to the turf.

The ridge spills onto Langstrath above Black-moss Pot, one of the best swimming holes in the Lake District. After some eight hours on the hoof you may be ready for a cooling dip. Others may prefer to steel themselves for another three stony miles down the valley for beer or a brew in Stonethwaite. *Corvus* and the day's round should have given you something to crow about.

CORVUS & CAM CRAG RIDGE

DISTANCE: 12km **TOTAL ASCENT:** 925m **START:** Lane near Stonethwaite GR: NY 261139 **TIME:** 8hrs
CLIMBING: *Corvus*, 157m, Diff **SCRAMBLING:** *Cam Crag Ridge*, in descent, *c.*-250m, Grade 2
MAP: OS Explorer OL4: The English Lakes North-western area, 1:25000 **REFRESHMENTS:** Langstrath Inn, Stonethwaite (T: 017687 77239); Peathouse tearoom, Stonethwaite; Riverside Bar at Scafell Hotel, Rosthwaite (T: 017687 77208); Shepherd's 'Caff' at High Lodore Farm, near Grange

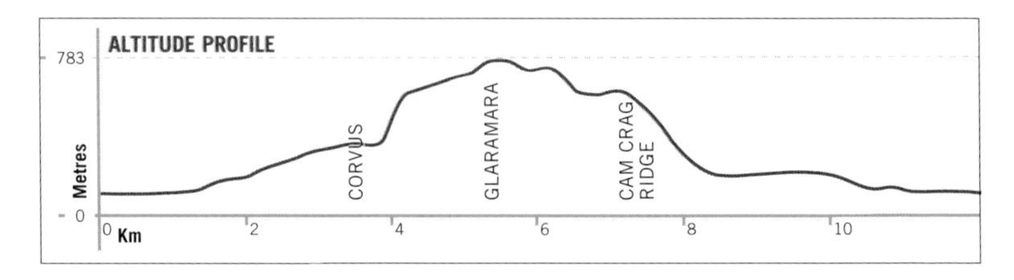

The Route **Corvus & Cam Crag Ridge**

Start

Lane near Stonethwaite. **GR: NY 261139.**

S Walk back up the lane towards the main road and turn left to pass Borrowdale Church and go through the farmyard.

2 A public footpath trends south-south-west by fields and lower fellside to the hanging valley of Combe Gill.

3 Cross the beck and briefly join the well-trodden path that heads up Thornythwaite Fell. At the cairn (270m), bear left off the main path and into the combe. Raven Crag stands out to the right of the head of The Combe.

4 As the path becomes indistinct use whatever trods seem least arduous on the toil up to the foot of the crag (450m) – approx 1.5 hours from the church corner.

ROUTE CONTINUES OVERLEAF

01
Seatoller
High Doat
Longthwaite
Johnny Wood
Peat Howe
Stonethwaite
Stonethwaite Bridge
Cumbria Way
Heron Crag
Knotts
White Crag
Huddleston's Shop
Burthwaite Bridge
Folly Bridge (FB)
Mountain View
Strands Bridge
Seatoller Bridge
Nichol Dub
Old Mill Cottage
Thorneywaite Farm
BORROWDALE CP
Low Buck How
High Buck How
Broad Haystack
Bull Crag
Alisongrass Hoghouse
Alisongrass Crag
Hanging Haystack
High Knott
Bessyboot
Johnny House
Belt Knott
Racom Bands
The Combe
Thornythwaite Fell
Borrowdale Fells
Rosthwaite Fell
Rosthwaite Cam
Cop Knott
White Crag
Ivy Knott
Dovenest Crag
Great Hollow
Stickle Brow
Raven Crag
Blackmoss Pot
Cam Crag
Woof Stones
Langstrath
Sheepfold
Combe Head
Combe Door
Black Wall
Stonethwaite Fell
Thick Side
Blea Crag
Glaramara
Looking Steads
South Crag
Brown Crag
Swan Dub
Tray Dub
Heron Crag
Bull Crag
Lamper Knott
Sergeant's Crag
2
3
4
5
C
6
7
8
S
9

5 **C** *Corvus* **(157m, Diff, B. Beetham, 10 June 1950)**

Starts on clean grey slabs just left of *Tyro's Gully* – a prominent dark gash down the centre of the crag.

P1 20m: Climb slabs left of the gully. As these steepen at 15m, traverse right to the back of the gully – belay on a ledge on the right of the centre line.

P2 15m: Climb the left-hand gully wall via the left of two grooves splitting the wall. Pull over onto a commodious platform.

P3 12m: Traverse left on ledges. This pitch was compared by Beetham to the 'Vire à Bicyclette' on the Grépon. The ledges are generous, but even so still await a first bicycle ascent. Belay below a corner.

Raven Crag.

P4 27m: Climb the corner; this tightens to a chimney – a squeeze best avoided by the arête on the left. A slabby scoop leads to a belay in a bay.

P5 33m: Walk and scramble rightwards over vegetation to the foot of a rib; ascend this on pleasing holds to the base of a wall.

P6 10m: The celebrated 'Hand Traverse'. Step up onto the wall at the right-hand end and utilising the obvious lateral break traverse leftwards to pull onto a large shelf. Belay around the corner.

P7 40m: Climb up from the right side of the landing bay onto an easy-angled rib and then a scoop of clean rock leading to the top. This was traditionally done in two pitches, belaying before the scoop.

Stephen Venables sets out on the *Corvus* 'Hand Traverse'.

6 From the top of the climb at *c*.550m follow the left side of a broken wall up to a gully and continue up its rocky bed to the fell. Head west over boggy ground to soon join the main felltop path (15 minutes from the top of the climb). Follow the felltop path roughly south for approximately 30 minutes and scramble up the final rocks to the summit of Glaramara (783m).

7 The top of *Cam Crag Ridge* lies 1.5km north-east of Glaramara. However, there is no direct path. The simplest way is to leave the summit of Glaramara on a track heading north-north-east towards Rosthwaite Fell and bear right off this in a boggy level at *c*.600m (before the main path rises again). Faint tracks trend east onto the broad top of the ridge.

8 **S** ***Cam Crag Ridge*** **(in descent, *c*.-250m, Grade 2)**

Follow the top of the ridge to where it steepens, overlooking Langstrath. The cleanest rock is on the nose of the ridge. Difficulties can be adjusted to taste using grass terraces and ledges, generally on the right of the nose in descent.

9 From the jumble of large boulders (Woof Stones) at the foot of the ridge, descend to the track and gate by Blackmoss Pot. Follow the track north down Langstrath to Stonethwaite.

Both photos: Scrambling par excellence on *Cam Crag Ridge* (climber Stephen Venables).

Eric Parker scrambling on Doves' Nest. This airy move is shared with the top pitch of *Face Route*.

02 **Intake Ridge & Doves' Nest Circuit**

7km Diff

A varied ridge scramble and a climb of subterranean novelty

STONETHWAITE – BORROWDALE CHURCH – THE COMBE (also known as Combe Gill) – *Intake Ridge*, Grade 2 – **DOVES' NEST** (*Face Route*, Diff) – **ROSTHWAITE FELL – BESSYBOOT – STANGER GILL – STONETHWAITE**

The day

As with *Corvus* (Route 1), this is another day in the nailed-bootsteps of the schoolteacher Bentley Beetham. Apparently he was a hard taskmaster in the classroom and could be a bit of brute to timorous lads on the crag, but he certainly had a nose for ferreting out interesting routes. The hanging valley of The Combe was Bentley's happy hunting ground and these two of his creations – *Intake Ridge* and *Face Route* – are gems of contrasting character. Together they offer a not-too-serious day of serendipitous exploration.

Face Route on Doves' Nest is also known as *Outside Route* but since its most memorable moves are made anything but 'outside', I will stick to its alias. As you squirm through the bowels of the crag, even *Face Route* may come to seem a misnomer.

There is no settled grade for *Intake Ridge* or agreement on its length. Nor is it an obvious 'ridge', more a series of craglets and grassy breaks trending up towards Bessyboot. Beetham gave it Mod and an estimated length of 187 metres – right to the summit cairn. The FRCC graded it Diff and cut the route short at 111 metres, where the best of the rock peters out.

The truth is the craglets offer so much scope to pick your own line – and that's the fun of it – that *Intake Ridge* is beyond definition. I regard it as a scramble, but it certainly is possible to link together a few steep Diff moves – particularly on the crag at half height above the delightful ice-smoothed outcrop called the Glaciated Slab – and then a rope could be desirable.

Rather than continue over the final craglets, we traverse the fellside to the geological oddity of Doves' Nest. In the distant past a huge piece of cliff has broken away, slid and then slumped back against the hillside, in the process creating a labyrinth of passageways and chimneys. More recent slippages have led to doubts about exploring too deeply – be warned. Luckily *Face Route* and others that do not stray far from the daylight have remained sound.

Beetham, who was in the first ascent party in 1944, described the rocks of Doves' Nest as affording 'a surprising amount of exercise and entertainment within a very small area'. Puzzling and strenuous in parts, but always engaging, *Face Route* makes the very best of it. Then we head over the fells and down to Stonethwaite by the steep stair of Stanger Gill.

INTAKE RIDGE & DOVES' NEST CIRCUIT

DISTANCE: 7km **TOTAL ASCENT:** 650m **START:** Lane near Stonethwaite GR: NY 261139 **TIME:** 6.5hrs
CLIMBING: *Face Route*, 70m, Diff **SCRAMBLING:** *Intake Ridge*, 170m, grade varies depending on route choices, typically 2, optional Diff **MAP:** OS Explorer OL4: The English Lakes North-western area, 1:25000
REFRESHMENTS: Langstrath Inn, Stonethwaite (T: 017687 77239); Peathouse tearoom, Stonethwaite; Riverside Bar at Scafell Hotel, Rosthwaite (T: 017687 77208); Shepherd's 'Caff' at High Lodore Farm, near Grange

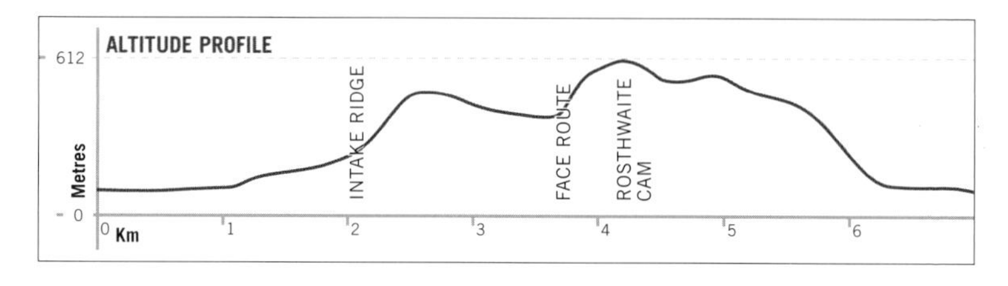

The Route
Intake Ridge & Doves' Nest Circuit

Start

Laneside parking on the approach to Stonethwaite. (Turn left off the Borrowdale road 700 metres south of Rosthwaite.) **GR: NY 261139.**

S **As for Route 1:** walk back up the lane towards the main road and turn left to pass Borrowdale Church and go through the farmyard. A public footpath trends south-south-west by fields and the lower fellside to the hanging valley of The Combe, also known as Combe Gill.

2 After passing through the last wall into The Combe turn left up the hillside. (**Route 1** turns right here and crosses the beck.) After about 15 minutes you reach a large ash tree growing out of boulders close to the wall.

ROUTE CONTINUES OVERLEAF

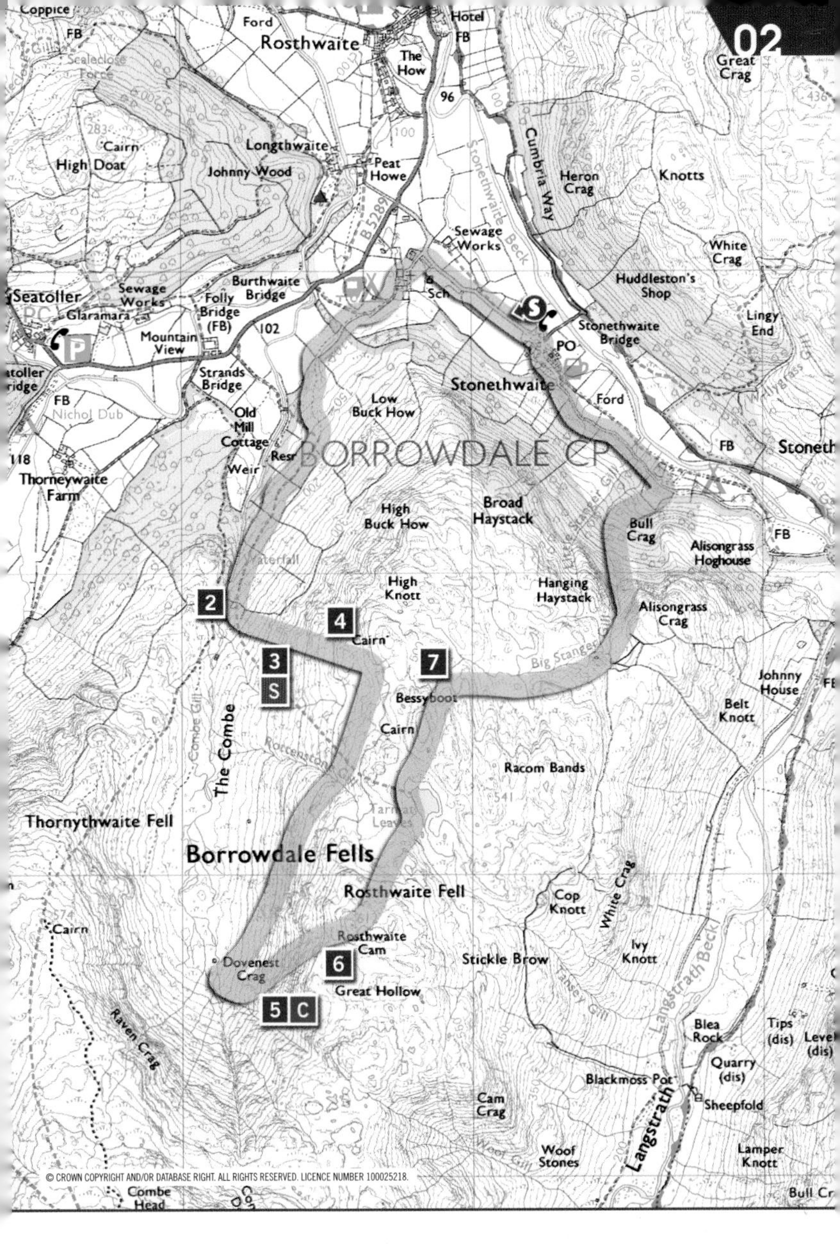
Rosthwaite
Hotel
The How
Longthwaite
Johnny Wood
High Doat
Peat Howe
Seatoller
Sewage Works
Burthwaite Bridge
Folly Bridge (FB)
Glaramara
Mountain View
Strands Bridge
Old Mill Cottage
Weir
Stonethwaite
Stonethwaite Bridge
Cumbria Way
Heron Crag
Knotts
White Crag
Huddleston's Shop
Lingy End
Low Buck How
BORROWDALE CP
High Buck How
Broad Haystack
Bull Crag
Alisongrass Hoghouse
High Knott
Hanging Haystack
Alisongrass Crag
Cairn
Bessyboot
Thorneywaite Farm
The Combe
Racom Bands
Thornythwaite Fell
Borrowdale Fells
Rosthwaite Fell
Rosthwaite Cam
Dovenest Crag
Great Hollow
Stickle Brow
Cop Knott
Ivy Knott
Raven Crag
Blackmoss Pot
Sheepfold
Cam Crag
Woof Stones
Langstrath
Langstrath Beck
Lamper Knott
Johnny House
Belt Knott
Blea Rock
Quarry (dis)
Tips (dis)
Combe Head
2
3
S
4
5
C
6
7

3 **S** ***Intake Ridge*** **(170m, Grade 2, B. Beetham, 1937)**

Scrambling begins at a spur of rock up and right of the ash tree. Ascend the left corner or descend slightly to the foot of the rock for a harder start. Trend rightwards, then across grass, to a longer spur which is followed to the rounded bare cap above Glaciated Slab. (This south-facing facet is good place to practise your slab climbing technique on a string of Diff lines, up to about 30m.)

From the top of the slab, cross scree and grass to a low spur, trending rightwards to the foot of a broken, heather-sprouting buttress and the most challenging moments on *Intake Ridge*. The bold, or roped, can step up to a heathery ramp and ascend steeply on good holds to gain the slabby stairway above. Easier alternatives start just to the left.

4 Outcrops continue intermittently towards Bessyboot, but unless you're a Beetham purist it is best to cease with the 'ridge' when the scrambling wanes at around the 470-metre contour and traverse south towards Doves' Nest. There is no path hereabouts and newcomers should get out the map and work out an approximate line; try not to lose height before crossing the trench of Rottenstone Gill. Descend gradually after the gill and work round below broken cliffs to the foot of the deeply fissured Doves' Nest crag. This takes approximately 45 minutes from *Intake Ridge*.

Dove's Nest, Borrowdale.

5 **C** ***Face*** **or** ***Outside Route*** **(70m, Diff, R.S.T. Chorley, B. Beetham, R.W. Somervell, 1944)**

Note: *Given the restrictions of the Central Chimney, it is prudent to leave sacks at the foot of Face Route and return for them down the gully to the south side of the crag. Re-ascent can then be made with a Grade 3 scramble up the right-hand side of the crag, following a corner and grooves before moving left to 'stubby pinnacle' near the top of the Face Route.*

Start at the right-hand side of the bulging slab that forms the lowest part of the crag.

P1 20m: Follow the obvious crack that slants leftwards up the slab to a big ledge. From the right end of the ledge, climb the arête to another big ledge below the North Chimney and then walk right along the ledge to below the South Chimney.

P2 8m: Here the climbing starts to become unusual. To your left is a large detached block. Climb this on good holds then walk along its crest towards the left end and belay where the Central Chimney leers from across a deep chasm.

P3 12m: Step down into the chasm and then boldly across into the chimney. A sling can be placed below the belay (i.e. on the detached block side of the chasm) to protect the second's descent and then removed just before stepping over to the chimney. Climb the chimney by whatever line suits your physique and abilities; it is a little less inelegant to stay on the outer side of the chockstones, and less grubby. Belay below the Attic Cave on top of a big chockstone.

P4 30m: Go up the rib on the left, take a big stride rightwards across the top of the chimney, and then go right a metre or so on slabs. Crack lines, good holds and clean rock lead enjoyably to a stubby pinnacle. Stride across left from the pinnacle and go easily up to the top.

6 From the top of Doves' Nest head north-north-east over intermittent slabs to the knobbly top of Rosthwaite Cam (612m), and then northwards, skirting the west shore of the tranquil Tarn at Leaves and on to Bessyboot.

7 Looking from the north edge of Bessyboot, pick out the faint grassy path that swings eastwards round the boggy ground at the head of Stanger Beck. This path can then be followed all the way down Stanger Gill to the track that leads into Langstrath. Here you are only 500m south of Stonethwaite and perhaps in need of refreshment at the Langstrath Inn.

Great End's gaping gullies.

03 **Ruddy Gill & Great End Circuit**

10km Mod/Diff

By pools, cascades and steep gullies

SEATHWAITE – STOCKLEY BRIDGE – *Ruddy Gill*, Grade 3 – *Central* or *Cust's* gully, both Mod – **GREAT END – SEATHWAITE FELL – SEATHWAITE**

The day

Come the days of snow and ice, climbers flock to the gullies and buttresses of Great End. Come spring and summer, the same north-east face is largely ignored. True, the *Central Gully* that climbers queue up in winter looks less attractive, with a strong suggestion of loose stones and wet rock. But persevere, there is sport for the adventurous in *Central Gully*, and also in *Cust's Gully* – indeed this unusual chasm is more of a challenge snowless than when it banks out in winter to become utterly benign.

Both gullies finish close to the top of 910-metre Great End, one of the finest vantage points in the Lake District. And either makes a satisfying main course after scrambling up from Borrowdale by the pools and cascades of Ruddy Gill.

A dry spell of weather – the longer the better – is needed for this outing, otherwise you will be too frequently forced out of Ruddy Gill and the rock of the two gullies could be extremely slippery. **A helmet is also strongly recommended** – *Central Gully* is loaded with loose scree. This is the reason neither of these gullies has found favour with earlier guidebook writers. *Central Gully* is the more serious and a rope and light rack should be taken. A rope might also be a comfort in *Cust's Gully*, depending on confidence and competence; a 25-metre scrambling rope would be ideal.

Yet the requirement for constant attention – tiptoeing in places, and trying to protect awkward moves on greasy rock – is what gives the routes their edge. They are not romps up dry slabs. You have to think a bit, the rope languishing in your pack will suddenly be called upon, and you'll emerge from the shadows on to Great End's summit with a feeling of satisfaction – it was neither as grim nor as easy as expected.

Great End forms the northern escarpment of the Scafell massif and commands fine views down Borrowdale to Skiddaw and Blencathra, and closer to hand to the head of Wasdale, to Great Gable and The Napes. In Neolithic times the summit area was also the site of a stone axe 'factory' – a subsidiary, perhaps, of the more celebrated axe factory on Pike of Stickle, six kilometres to the east.

After descending to Sprinkling Tarn, there is a choice of routes for the return to Seathwaite. If you're ready to switch off from route finding and just coast down, then the optional route along the broad highway via Styhead Tarn is the easiest. Otherwise, our less trodden way lies directly north from Sprinkling Tarn over Seathwaite Fell, a quiet upland of hummocks and glassy pools.

RUDDY GILL & GREAT END CIRCUIT

DISTANCE: 10km **TOTAL ASCENT:** *c.*900m **START:** Seathwaite Farm GR: NY 235122 **TIME:** 6.5hrs
CLIMBING: *Central Gully*, 180m, Mod/Diff, short section merits a rope; *Cust's Gully*, *c.*80m, Grade 3/Mod
SCRAMBLING: *Ruddy Gill*, 300m, Grade 2 **MAP:** OS Explorers OL4 & OL6: The English Lakes North-western & South-western areas, 1:25000 **REFRESHMENTS:** Riverside Bar at Scafell Hotel, Rosthwaite (T: 017687 77208); Shepherd's 'Caff' at High Lodore Farm, near Grange

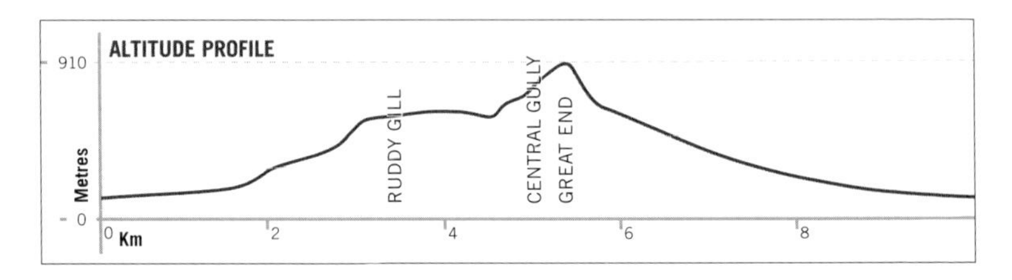

The Route
Ruddy Gill & Great End Circuit

Start

Laneside parking on the approach to Seathwaite, before Seathwaite Farm. (Turn left off the Borrowdale road just before Seatoller.) On busy weekends parked cars can back up for half a mile. **GR: NY 187085.**

S→ Walk through Seathwaite Farm and south along the main track to Stockley Bridge.

2 After crossing the bridge, go through a gate and turn immediately left to follow the path up Grains.

3 About 1km from Stockley Bridge the beck is crossed on a footbridge. Leave the path here and follow the streambed. Scrambling soon begins. (If there is too much water in the beck or time is tight, stay with the path. Either way will lead to **Point 4**.)

ROUTE CONTINUES OVERLEAF

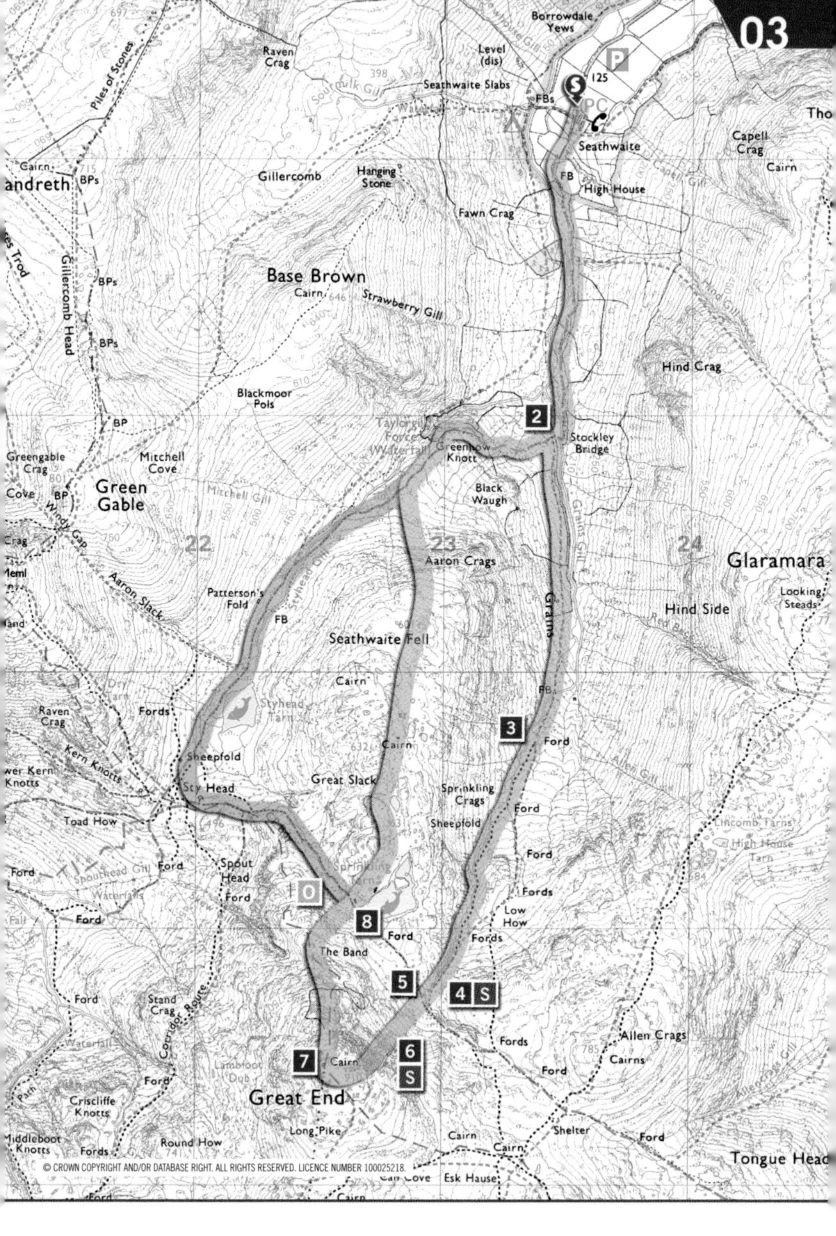
03
Borrowdale Yews
Raven Crag
Level (dis)
Piles of Stones
Seathwaite Slabs
Sourmilk Gill
125
FBs
Seathwaite
Thorn
Capell Crag
Cairn
Gillercomb
Hanging Stone
FB
High House
Fawn Crag
Gillercomb Head
BPs
Base Brown
Cairn
Strawberry Gill
Hind Crag
Blackmoor Pols
BP
Taylorgill Force Waterfall
Greenhow Knott
Stockley Bridge
Greengable Crag
Mitchell Cove
Green Gable
Black Waugh
Windy Gap
Mitchell Gill
22
23
24
Aaron Crags
Glaramara
Aaron Slack
Patterson's Fold
FB
Grains Gill
Hind Side
Looking Steads
Seathwaite Fell
Cairn
Raven Crag
Fords
Styhead Tarn
FBs
Ford
Sheepfold
Kern Knotts
Cairn
Great Slack
Sty Head
Sprinkling Crags
Ford
Allen Gill
Toad How
Sheepfold
Lincomb Tarns
High House Tarn
Spout Head
Ford
Fords
Low How
The Band
Fords
Stand Crag
Corridor Route
Allen Crags
Cairns
Cairn
Great End
Ford
Criscliffe Knotts
Long Pike
Shelter
Middleboot Knotts
Fords
Round How
Cairn
Tongue Head
Esk Hause
Calf Cove
2
3
4
S
5
6
7
8
O

4 S *Ruddy Gill* (300m, Grade 2)

Ruddy Gill presents the scrambler with an easy classic of the genre: cascades with water-cleansed slabs to either side, pools to circumvent and shadowed clefts where the rock remains perpetually greasy. The art, as ever, is to keep as close to the water course as possible without getting wet. Where the risk of soaking becomes too great, *Ruddy Gill* offers bypasses up the bank.

The scrambling is not continuous and the path can be rejoined for the walk up to the deeply incised upper ravine, the trickiest part of the gully. Where an enclosed pool and cascade appear to bar the way, search for good holds on the right wall and boldly go. The forbidding top pool is usually avoided by muttering 'discretion is the better part of valour' and scrabbling up a chute on the right bank.

Entering the depths of Ruddy Gill.

Ron Kenyon approaches the crux in *Central Gully*.

5 Here, where the Grains path meets the well-trodden Wasdale-Langdale highway, the north-east face of Great End looms directly ahead. Two gully lines stand out. *Central Gully* is the widest, trending slightly rightwards and splitting halfway up the face. To its left, taking a straighter line, is *South-east Gully*, a great winter route but not for us today. *Cust's Gully* lies out of sight at the right-hand (west) edge of the crag. For either *Central* or *Cust's*, ascend to the base of *Central Gully*. There are trodden zigzags either side of the scree chute issuing from *Central Gully*.

6 **S** ***Central Gully*** **(180m, Mod/Diff, W.P. Haskett-Smith, 1882)**

The first half of the gully is straightforward scrambling over blocks and up rubble. Where the gully is split by a high fin of rock, take the right-hand fork. The crux comes below a 'V' corner where a high step across must be made (*right-hand photo, opposite page*). This move can be protected by a high nut placement. Pull across and continue up rightwards into the upper scree-filled gully.

Great End.

O **S** ***Cust's Gully* (c.80m, Grade 3/Mod)**

From the foot of *Central Gully* traverse up rightwards along the base of the crag to its western corner. *Cust's* is a distinctive cleft with a giant chockstone poised atop its near-vertical sidewalls. The crux is a chockstone in the gully bed above a steep step. Climb delicately up the right-hand wall and squeeze beneath the chockstone. Above, the gully exit appears blocked, but a pile of rocks on the right-hand side lead up to the final scree chute.

7 Both gullies finish at the top of the crag with Great End summit (910m) just a short way to the right. Descend northwards from the summit on a steep path, skittery in places and sometimes wayward. Styhead Tarn is the best point to aim for, though the path, once located, swings rightward.

Great End.

8 For the Seathwaite Fell route, take a bee-line north-east for Sprinkling Tarn once off steep ground, skirt the left side of the tarn and follow an indistinct path northwards over the fell to Aaron Crags. A shallow depression to the north-west offers the easiest descent to join the main Styhead Gill path to Stockley Bridge and Seathwaite.

The descent route above from Aaron Crags passes several fissured slabs where a few minutes' play is hard to resist …

O Alternatively, from **Point 8** follow the main Wasdale-Langdale path north-west to Sty Head and at the junction turn right (north-north-east) to pass Styhead Tarn and carry on down for 2km to Stockley Bridge.

In *Central Gully.* Beware loose stones.

Waterfall wonders in *Sourmilk Gill* (climber Alan Davis).

04 Sourmilk Gill & Grey Knotts Face

7km Hard Diff

An entertaining day's climbing by cascades and a puzzling 'letter box'

SEATHWAITE – *Sourmilk Gill*, Grade 3 – **SEATHWAITE SLABS** – **GILLERCOMB** – *Grey Knotts Face*, Hard Diff – **BRANDRETH** – **GREEN GABLE** – **GILLERCOMB** – **SEATHWAITE**

The day

Code words and euphemisms have long been a feature of climbing guides. Usually they tend to understatement and a keen appreciation of this can avoid uncomfortable surprises. What exactly did Bentley Beetham mean when in the FRCC's 1953 *Borrowdale* guide he described the so-called 'letter box' on *Grey Knotts Face* as 'an interesting and unusual pitch'?

'Interesting' is always a word to be wary of. However in the case of the *Grey Knotts Face* later FRCC scribes have been less opaque: 'Not recommended for stout persons,' is the warning. From my observation, thin but tall persons also find the contortions of the 'letter box' a challenge. Indeed probably the only individuals likely to romp through it are those with the physique of the child labourers of early Victorian chimney sweeps.

But don't let any of this deter you. The water-scoured slabs and stairs of *Sourmilk Gill* followed by the cracks and chimneys of *Grey Knotts Face* make for an ascent of almost constant entertainment – no euphemism intended! And all this set gloriously at the head of Borrowdale with the modest summit of Brandreth to round off the day.

A big plus for *Sourmilk Gill* is that the scrambling begins only fifteen minutes after leaving the car. And though the gill is fringed in ash and birch and holly, it has an open aspect, sun dappling the cascades and much of the rock quick to dry. With plenty of scope to choose your own line, the grade can be varied from easy scrambling to occasional moves at Moderate or Difficult.

Close by the top waterfall are the Upper Seathwaite Slabs; as fun is the order of the day, pause here and hone your balancing skills, padding up the easy-angled rock. Then it is on to the impressive crag that stands in full view fifteen minutes' walk across the floor of Gillercomb. Though named 'Raven Crag' on the OS map, climbers tend to refer to it as 'Gillercombe Buttress', after the classic route of the crag (a worthy objective but at Severe just above the grade for this book).

The fabled 'letter box' is a slit that gives entry to a 'crevasse' behind a wall of rock that has separated a foot or so from the main cliff. But while this pitch is likely to prove the most memorable part of the climb, there is interest throughout. As height is gained, the climber looks out from chimney cracks and broken arêtes over Gillercomb to much of the Lake District. The panorama is completed shortly after coiling ropes. Walk to the skyline and the view to the west opens out, ideally as the sun dips to the Irish Sea.

SOURMILK GILL & GREY KNOTTS FACE

DISTANCE: 7km **TOTAL ASCENT:** *c.*700m **START:** Seathwaite farm GR: NY 235122 **TIME:** 6.5–7hrs
CLIMBING: *Grey Knotts Face*, 170m, Hard Diff **SCRAMBLING:** *Sourmilk Gill*, 220m, max Grade 3
MAP: OS Explorer OL4: The English Lakes North-western area, 1:25000 **REFRESHMENTS:** Riverside Bar at Rosthwaite (T: 017687 77208); Shepherd's 'Caff' at High Lodore farm, near Grange

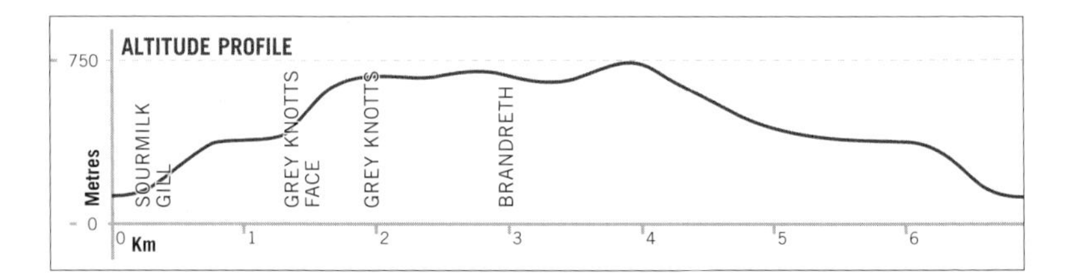

The Route
Sourmilk Gill & Grey Knotts Face

Start

Laneside parking on the approach to Seathwaite. (Turn left off the Borrowdale road just before Seatoller.) Park on the side of the lane before Seathwaite farm. On busy weekends parked cars can back up for half a mile. **GR: NY 235122.**

Walk to Seathwaite Farm and turn right in the yard under the arch. A path leads to a footbridge over Seathwaite Beck.

Sourmilk Gill begins soon after crossing the footbridge. Simply follow the bouldery streambed and soon arrive at the first falls, with a slab on the right. From here on, the degree of difficulty can be adjusted to your own taste, and to the amount of water cascading down.

2 S *Sourmilk Gill* (220m, max Grade 3)

For the first two-thirds of the ascent, the cleanest and most attractive rock is on the right of the stream. Nearing the top, a fence is crossed – most easily on the left – to reach a gothic amphitheatre with a high waterfall at its back and an isolated pillar in its centre. **Beware**: the pillar may be tempting, but down-climbing it is tricky with greasy footholds and worrying exposure.

Climb out of the amphitheatre via the left-hand wall, either on a rising traverse below a prominent ash tree to gain the crest of the wall, or, easier, ascending to the left of the tree onto grass and then rejoining the crest nearer the top of the waterfall. The scramble ends here on the lip of Gillercomb.

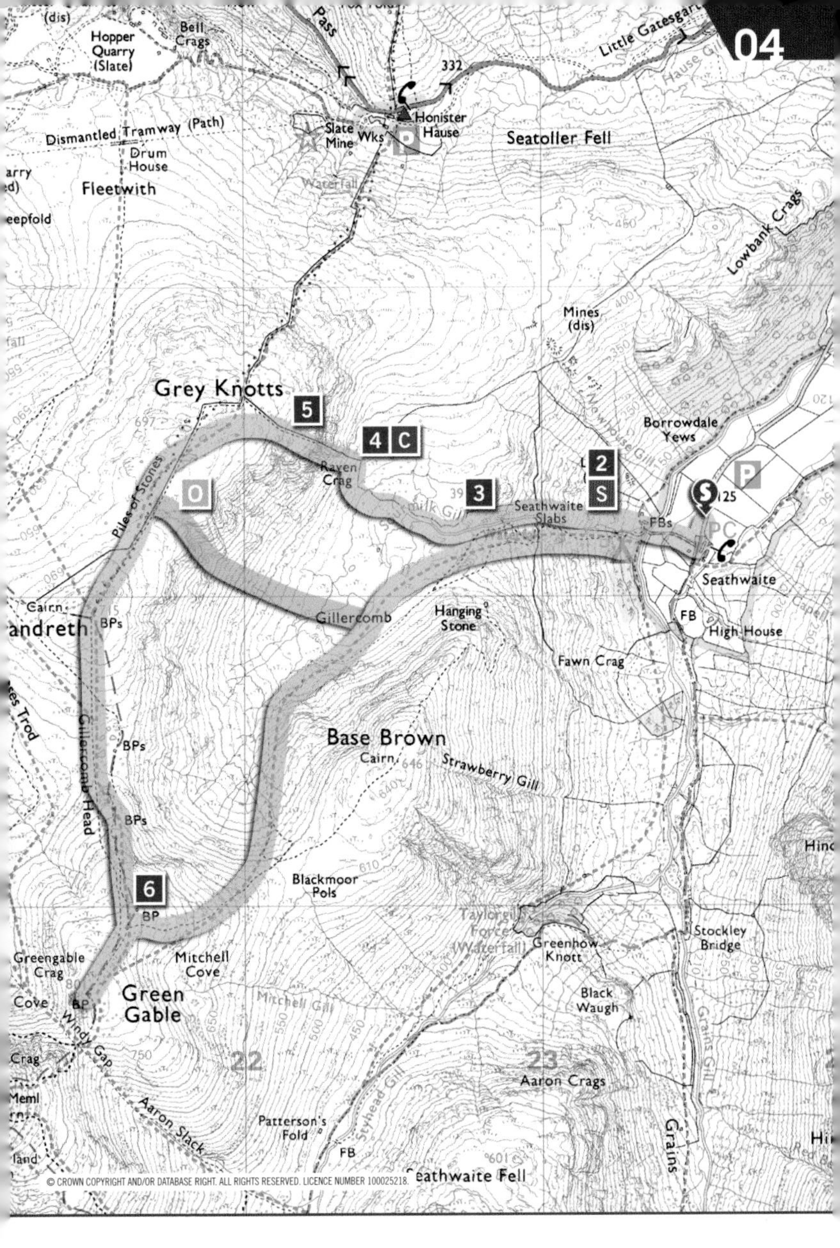
Grey Knotts
Raven Crag
Seathwaite Slabs
Seathwaite
Borrowdale Yews
Honister Hause
Seatoller Fell
Fleetwith
Dismantled Tramway (Path)
Drum House
Hopper Quarry (Slate)
Bell Crags
Slate Mine
Lowbank Crags
Mines (dis)
Piles of Stones
Gillercomb
Hanging Stone
High House
Fawn Crag
Base Brown
Strawberry Gill
Gillercomb Head
Blackmoor Pols
Taylorgill Force (Waterfall)
Greenhow Knott
Stockley Bridge
Mitchell Cove
Greengable Crag
Green Gable
Windy Gap
Aaron Slack
Black Waugh
Aaron Crags
Patterson's Fold
Seathwaite Fell
Grains Gill
Styhead Gill
Mitchell Gill

3 From the top of the falls, the cliffs that form the eastern edge of Grey Knotts rise directly ahead across the moor, with our intended route straight up their centre. But before setting out across the moor, sample the delightful Upper Seathwaite Slabs, just over a ladder stile on the north side of the beck. The coarse-grained, easy-angled slabs can be climbed anywhere up to a grade of about V Diff.

Playtime over, walk west-north-west over the moor, aiming for a fence descending from the foot of the crag. It is barely 15 minutes from the falls to the start of the Grey Knotts climb.

4 **C** ***Grey Knotts Face*** **(170m, Hard Diff, B. Beetham 1939)**

The complete route, as essayed by Bentley Beetham, begins below the main crag on a low outcrop that gives one long Moderate **P1** to boulders; then follow the fence to the foot of the main crag.

Gillercombe Buttress.

P2 25m: Easy rocks to a large grass ledge, then diagonally rightwards over rock and vegetation to a corner below the chimney; holly tree on the left.

P3 25m: Go awkwardly up blocks to beneath 'the letter box'. Take off your rucksack and slot it through on the right into the 'crevasse' behind the massive block, pushing the sack upwards to lodge a little higher. Now climb though the letter box – **facing out** from the crag – and thrutch up the crevasse, hauling rucksack, to land on the top of the block. From the left end of block, climb the chimney/crack and continue to a belay in a grassy bay; nut placements at the back of the bay.

P4 30m: Stepped rock left of the bay leads to a chimney crack; continue past a ledge (possible belay) and chockstone to grass and heather (try not to get too embedded in the chimney). Belay at the base of the groove.

P5/6 60m: The remainder of the route gives easy climbing/scrambling, either moving together or in two pitches. Follow the line of the groove or, better still, the clean rock to its right.

No place for the portly! Squeezing out of the 'letter box' on *Grey Knotts Face* (climber Paul Goulding).

5 From the top of the climb, walk up to the skyline and the summit of Grey Knotts (697m). Follow a cairned path along the broad ridge south-west to Brandreth (715m) and then south to a path junction at the head of Gillercomb, just before the final rise to Green Gable.

O If time or energy is running out after the climb, a short cut can be made east from the col between Grey Knotts and Brandreth, descending steep grass and crossing the floor of Gillercomb to join the homeward path on the far side of the comb.

6 From the head of Gillercomb (*c.*760m), the summit of Green Gable (801m), just a short ascent south-west, is an option. Otherwise turn left (east) and descend steadily north-east into the comb; it is 2km to the top of Sourmilk Gill. The footpath continues down on the south side of the gill to rejoin the outward route at the footbridge over Seathwaite Beck.

Steve Prior romping up *Sourmilk Gill.*

What goes up must come down. Be warned: this pillar by *Sourmilk Gill* can be tricky to down-climb.

The author on pitch 2 of *Needle Ridge*, with Napes Needle behind and Wasdale Head beyond. Photo: Phil Blanshard.

05 Needle Ridge Circuit

11km V Diff

A classic in the cradle of rock climbing

HONISTER HAUSE – MOSES TROD – CLIMBERS' TRAVERSE – THE NAPES (*Needle Ridge*, V Diff) – **WESTMORLAND CRAGS** (*Pinnacle Ridge*, Grade 2) – **GREAT GABLE – GREEN GABLE – BRANDRETH – HONISTER HAUSE**

The day

The Napes, Wasdale. Other crags can, with honour, claim earlier ascents, but this is where rock climbing really took off. Napes is climbing's raw-edged cradle. And *Needle Ridge* was the first ascent to be made there, in 1884 by W.P. Haskett-Smith, two years before he climbed the eponymous Needle.

It was the sheer photogenic quality of the free-standing Needle that caught the attention of the Victorian climbers to-be. Haskett-Smith's daring solo of the pinnacle was featured in the *Pall Mall Gazette* in 1890 – nothing like a bit of publicity down in London – and O.G. Jones was fired up by a picture of the Needle in a shop on the Strand. From consequent forays north came Jones's influential *Rock Climbing in the English Lake District*.

On this outing you will literally rub shoulders with the Needle before tackling the generally more amenable ridge above. The qualification there is necessary as the first moves on *Needle Ridge* up a short slab will test your nerve. The slab is just a little too steep to stay comfortably in balance on, while such edges as there are have become rounded and polished by the passage of countless questing hands and boots.

In retrospect though, the slab becomes the piquant moment in a day of delightful movement on sound rock, accompanied throughout by long views to the west over Ennerdale and Wasdale.

Starting the day from the slate mine on Honister Hause saves a bit of uphill effort compared to valley approaches to Napes, but even so this is a long day. The outward walk traverses the head of Ennerdale and passes beneath Gable Crag, an imposing north-facing cliff with a famous hard route up its centre – *Engineer's Slabs*. The path you're following here is known as Moses' Trod – allegedly used by the said Moses in his illicit whisky business.

There's no conjecture about the origins of the rocky route followed around the foot of The Napes to *Needle Ridge*. The 'Climbers' Traverse' has been trodden by generations of climbers heading for a host of classic routes up the ridges and walls of the Napes. While *Needle Ridge* is the main course for the day, from its top a natural continuation leading almost to the summit of Great Gable lays only a few minutes' walk away, taking you to *Pinnacle Ridge*, a Grade 2 scramble up Gable's southern rampart, Westmorland Crags.

The day will probably be drawing on as you pause by the memorial to the war dead of the Fell & Rock that stands on the summit of Great Gable. And it's still a good long walk back to Honister Hause. With luck though, you will be blessed with the final pleasure of the Honister approach to the Napes – the sun going down over the Irish Sea as you hike the broad ridge over Green Gable and Brandreth. Quite a day!

NEEDLE RIDGE CIRCUIT

DISTANCE: 11km **TOTAL ASCENT:** 850m **START:** Slate mine car park GR: NY 225136 **TIME:** 8–9hrs **CLIMBING:** *Needle Ridge c.*105m, V Diff **SCRAMBLING** *Pinnacle Ridge c.*50m, Grade 2 **MAP:** OS Explorer OL4: The English Lakes North-western area, 1:25000 **REFRESHMENTS:** Pubs and cafés at Buttermere and in Borrowdale

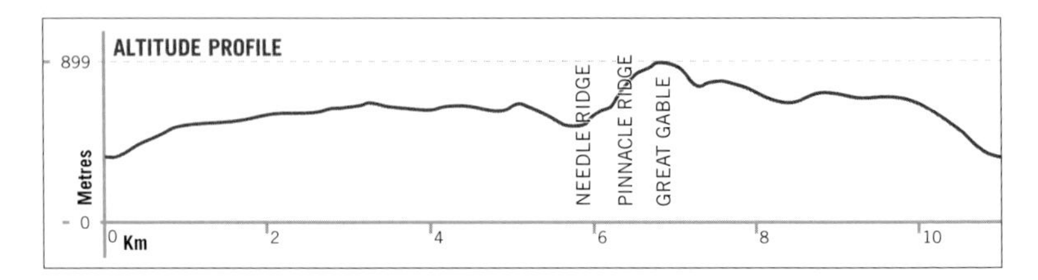

The Route **Needle Ridge Circuit**

Start

Honister Hause (on the pass between Borrowdale and Buttermere). Pay parking at the Honister slate mine and in the National Trust car park behind the youth hostel. **GR: NY 225136.**

S From the slate mine car park, a mine road leads west towards the workings and Fleetwith Pike. Follow this for about 200m, then bear off left up a path that skirts a wall and then follows the raised course of a dismantled tramway westwards up the fell.

2 On reaching the broad crest of the fell at a point named on the OS map as 'Drum House' (a ruined foundation), turn left and follow a broad, cairned path southwards along the west flank of Grey Knotts and Brandreth. This then dips into Stone Cove below Windy Gap before rising to Beck Head at the foot of the north-west ridge of Great Gable. The path is marked as Moses Trod; it is about 4km from Drum House to Beck Head.

3 Beck Head is a col on the watershed between Ennerdale and Wasdale. Descend the path to Wasdale for about 5 minutes (*c.*200m in distance). At a cairn atop a square block veer off left on an indistinct path to pick up a traverse line over bouldery scree to the foot of White Napes.

4 An airy path known as the 'Climbers' Traverse' skirts the foot of The Napes, beginning with the distinctive Sphinx Ridge. On rounding the ridge, ascend Sphinx Gully a short way, then traverse to a second gully, scramble up beside a short wall and cross to squeeze behind a large flake. Delicate traversing (grade 1 scrambling) leads to the 'Dress Circle', below Eagle's Nest Ridge. From here, the *Needle Ridge* climb is in full view, beginning from the notch or 'Gap' between the Needle pinnacle and the main crag. Descend to Needle Gully and climb the stepped corner to the Gap.

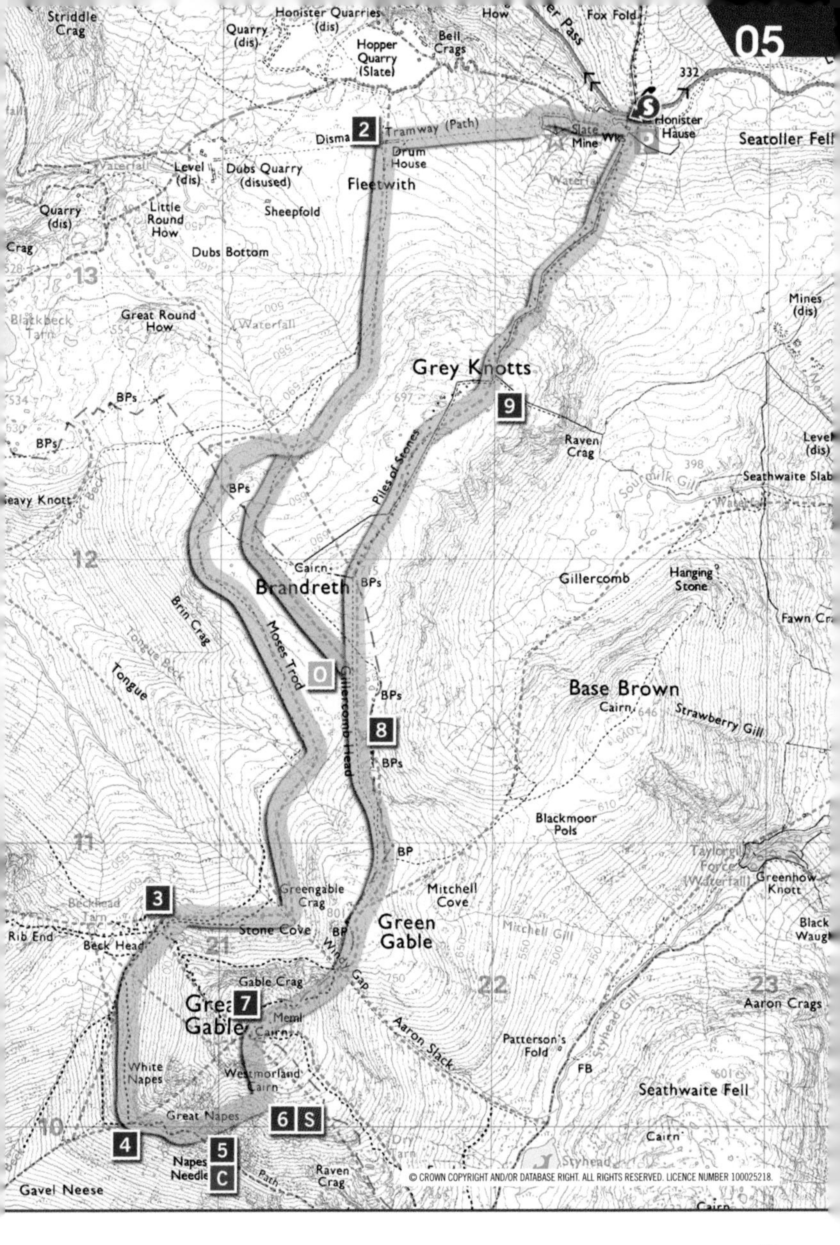
05
Striddle Crag
Honister Quarries (dis)
Quarry (dis)
Hopper Quarry (Slate)
Bell Crags
Fox Fold
332
Honister Hause
Seatoller Fell
2
Tramway (Path)
Drum House
Slate Mine
Level (dis)
Dubs Quarry (disused)
Fleetwith
Quarry (dis)
Little Round How
Sheepfold
Crag
Dubs Bottom
13
Great Round How
Blackbeck Tarn
Waterfall
Mines (dis)
Grey Knotts
9
BPs
Raven Crag
Level (dis)
398
Seathwaite Slab
Sourmilk Gill
Piles of Stones
Haystacks
12
Cairn
Brandreth
Gillercomb
Hanging Stone
Fawn Crag
Brin Crag
Moses Trod
Tongue Beck
Tongue
0
Gillercomb Head
Base Brown
Cairn
646
Strawberry Gill
8
610
Blackmoor Pols
11
BP
Taylorgill Force (Waterfall)
Greenhow Knott
3
Greengable Crag
Mitchell Cove
Beckhead Tarn
801
Green Gable
Rib End
Beck Head
Stone Cove
Windy Gap
Mitchell Gill
Black Waugh
21
Gable Crag
750
22
23
Great Gable
7
Aaron Slack
Aaron Crags
White Napes
Westmorland Cairn
Patterson's Fold
Styhead Gill
FB
Seathwaite Fell
Great Napes
6
S
10
4
5
Napes Needle
C
Path
Raven Crag
Dry Tarn
Cairn
Styhead
Gavel Neese
© CROWN COPYRIGHT AND/OR DATABASE RIGHT. ALL RIGHTS RESERVED. LICENCE NUMBER 100025218.

An easier approach after rounding Sphinx Ridge traverses scree and rocky nobbles to enter Needle Gully a short distance below the Needle itself. From here it appears as a sharply undercut square block rather than a needle. Ascend the gully to the foot of the corner below the Gap.

5 C *Needle Ridge* (105m, V Diff, W.P. Haskett Smith & J.W. Robinson, 1884)

P1 10m: Start up the slab directly above the Gap. The passage of countless hands and feet has rendered this the hardest bit of the route. Edges are rounded and polished, necessitating a delicate but positive approach. The slab can be outflanked to its right, but this is also awkward. Above the lip of the slab, trend left up a short groove to block belay on the ridge below a wall.

P2 15m: Climb the wall using the crack; continue up easier rocks to a block ledge and a stance beyond.

P3 15m: Climb the chimney above for a short stretch, then move left to an edge and continue up to a large ledge.

P4 30m: The groove above leads to the crest of the ridge; move left and climb a good crack in the wall overlooking Needle Gully.

Needle Ridge lower section.

Needle Ridge upper section.

P5 **35m:** Scramble along the blocky crest to the top of the ridge.

From the grassy shoulder above the Napes, angle down and across Great Hell Screes to the foot of Westmorland Crags, the obvious broken cliff that forms the southern rampart of Great Gable.

6 **S** ***Pinnacle Ridge*, Westmorland Crags (*c*.50m, Grade 2, FA by 1894)**

Start just right of a two-person high, square-cut boulder in the centre of the foot of the crag. The route follows a ragged staircase of steps and ledges trending leftwards. The 'pinnacle' is encountered about halfway up. Move left through the gap behind the pinnacle and climb a short wall to regain the crest. Scramble easily onwards to the top of the route. A short walk leads up to the summit of Great Gable and the FRCC memorial.

7 Great Gable (899m). Take care to get the right path off Gable. In poor visibility its stony dome can be confusing, with cairns marking several directions. Go north-east from the summit; once off the plateau the way is more obvious, winding steeply down towards Windy Gap. From here a short ascent gains Green Gable.

8 At the shallow col between Green Gable and Brandreth there is a choice: either continue along the watershed over Brandreth and Grey Knotts. **O** Alternatively, descend north-west on a gentle slope to rejoin the outward Moses Trod path and thence to Honister Hause.

9 Grey Knotts (697m). From this final summit of the round, follow the path alongside the wall descending roughly north-north-east and in 1km arrive at Honister Hause.

Westmorland Crags.

Gatesgarthdale from Grey Crag, Buttermere.

06 **Grey Crag Circuit**

8km Severe

The finest triptych in Lakeland - or make it a quartet

BUTTERMERE – BURTNESS (AKA BIRKNESS) COMB – GREY CRAG, (*Harrow Buttress*, Diff; *Slabs Ordinary*, V Diff; Oxford and Cambridge Buttress options) – **HIGH STILE – RED PIKE – BUTTERMERE**

The day

Grey Crag offers undoubtedly the finest link-up of easy-grade climbs in the Lake District. Three routes of increasing difficulty lead from the foot of the crag by way of buttresses, slabs and a superlative arête to the 807-metre summit of High Stile. It's a day to savour: clean rock, the atmosphere of a high mountain haven, and from almost every stance, a raven's view out over Buttermere and the fells of northern Lakeland.

Rising 150 metres in three disjointed tiers, Grey Crag faces roughly south-east across tranquil Birkness Comb to the shadowed mass of Eagle Crag – a towering buttress of far more serious mien; hard routes that shun the sun. (Though the comb is most popularly known as 'Birkness Comb', the Ordnance Survey persists with 'Burtness', a point for newcomers to be aware of when studying the map.)

This is a full-on rock climbing day so come equipped accordingly. No doubt the pioneers essayed these routes in nailed boots, but the crag's delightfully rough-textured Borrowdale volcanic is best enjoyed in rock shoes. And as well as a full set of wires and slings, two or three medium-sized cams are recommended, notably for the overhang on *Oxford and Cambridge Direct*.

Harrow Buttress, at the easier end of Diff, provides a good introduction to the crag, indeed to the craft of rock-climbing itself, on a route that dates back to pioneering days on Grey Crag before World War One.

Slabs Ordinary steps up a grade to V Diff, ascending an open face on Chockstone Buttress in the centre of the crag. First climbed in 1913, it is of similar vintage to *Harrow Buttress*, but fell into disuse after a dramatic rock fall in 1972. A 'piano-sized' block broke away with a climber on top of it; the roar was heard in the valley, but luckily all concerned survived. Thirty years later a slightly rearranged *Slabs Ordinary* was reopened to form the satisfying route of today.

Grey Crag reserves its *pièce de résistance* to the end – *Oxford and Cambridge Direct* is a forty-metre treat, its sense of exposure accentuated by the climber's sensational position on an arête at almost 800 metres poised, it seems, over half of Lakeland. True, at grade Severe, *Ox and Cambs Direct* is at the hard end for this guidebook, but the rock is perfect and by this point in the day you should have found a rhythm.

As suggested below, it is good idea to climb this one route without a pack, then descend a nearby gully, collect the pack and re-ascend the buttress via the easier *Oxford and Cambridge Ordinary Route*. However you play it, as the name of three of these routes suggests, the day will have provided a top class education in rock climbing.

GREY CRAG CIRCUIT

DISTANCE: 8km **TOTAL ASCENT:** 800m **START:** Bridge Hotel GR: NY 175170 **TIME:** 7.5hrs **CLIMBING:** *Harrow Buttress, Slabs Ordinary, Oxford and Cambridge Direct, Oxford and Cambridge Ordinary Route*, total 185m, max Severe **SCRAMBLING:** None **MAP:** OS Explorer OL4: The English Lakes North-western area, 1:25000 **REFRESHMENTS:** Croft House Farm Café (T: 017687 70235); Bridge Hotel (T: 017687 70252); Fish Hotel (T: 017687 70253); all at Buttermere

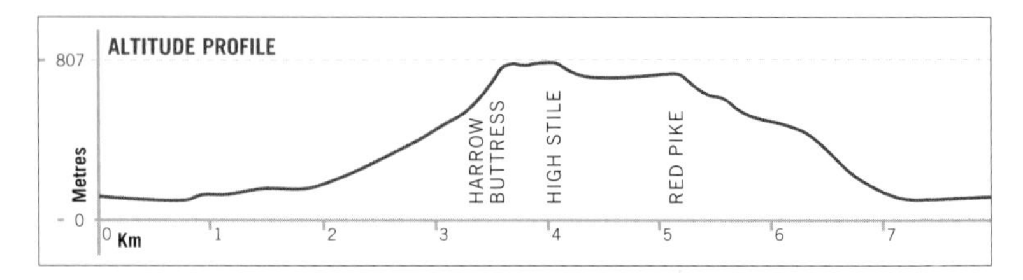

The Route **Grey Crag Circuit**

Start

Buttermere village, by the Bridge Hotel; there are various parking options in and around the village, including a pay and display car park behind the Fish Hotel. **GR: NY 175170.**

S From the Bridge Hotel follow the main path/farm road past the Fish Hotel and southwards towards the shore of Buttermere.

2 At the west corner of the lake cross two footbridges and follow the bridleway that skirts the south-west shore.

3 Roughly 700m from the footbridges a path bears off right, angling up and soon leaving the trees and following an indistinct path up into Burtness (Birkness) Comb.

***Note:** This was the best approach at the time of writing, however forestry operations sometimes affect these paths. A sure alternative is to follow either the forest track/bridleway or lakeside path to the south-east exit from Burtness Wood then turn right, directly up the hillside, to cross the wall by a ladder stile and join the indistinct path up into Burtness Comb.*

4 Continue up the floor of the comb on an intermittent path, curving westwards, with Eagle Crag high on the left and Grey Crag ahead above the scree slope. Ascend scree to the foot of the crag. (1 hour 40 minutes from the Bridge Inn.)

ROUTE CONTINUES OVERLEAF

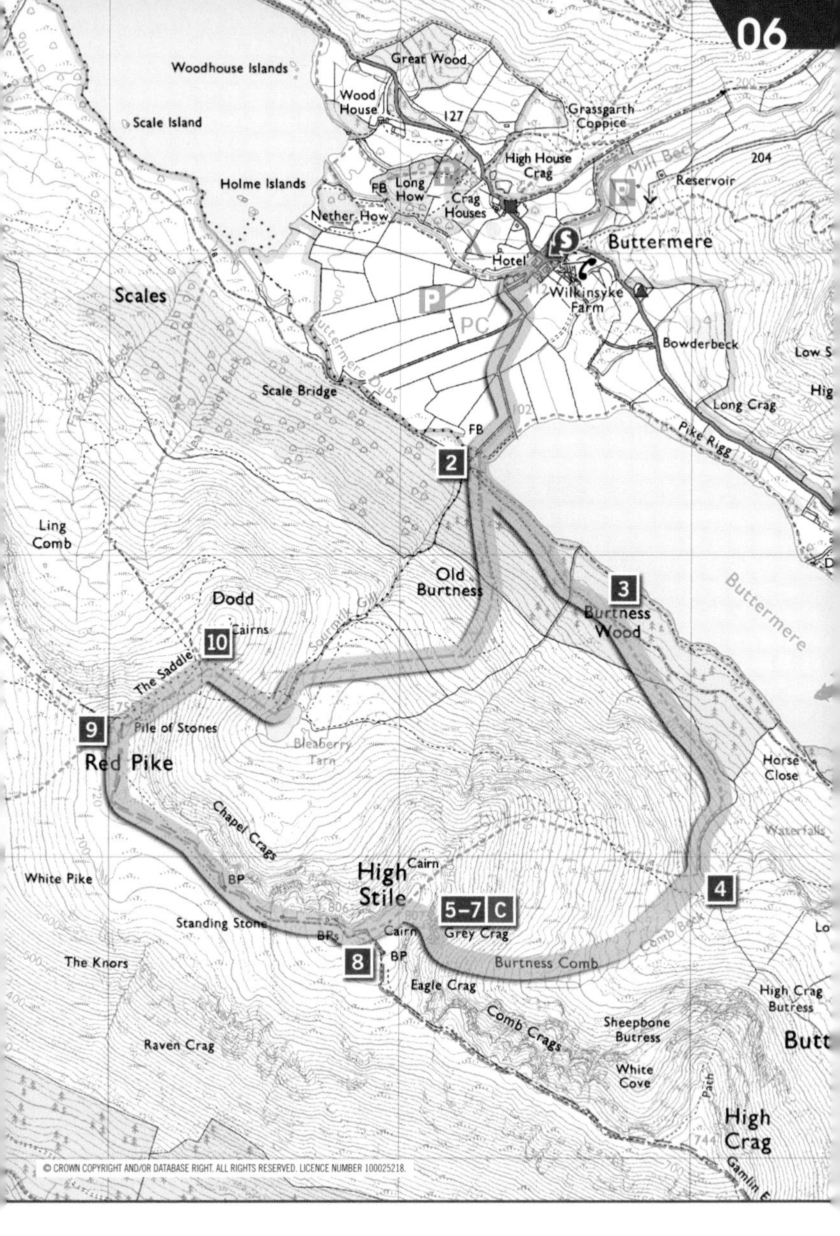
06
Woodhouse Islands
Great Wood
Wood House
127
Grassgarth Coppice
Scale Island
High House Crag
204
Mill Beck
Holme Islands
FB
Long How
Crag Houses
Reservoir
Nether How
Buttermere
Hotel
Wilkinsyke Farm
Scales
PC
Bowderbeck
Buttermere Dubs
Scale Bridge
Long Crag
FB
Pike Rigg
2
Ling Comb
Old Burtness
3
Burtness Wood
Dodd
Cairns
10
The Saddle
9
Pile of Stones
Bleaberry Tarn
Red Pike
Horse Close
Chapel Crags
Waterfalls
High Stile
Cairn
White Pike
BP
4
806
5–7
C
Standing Stone
BPs
Cairn
Grey Crag
Burtness Comb
Comb Beck
8
BP
The Knors
Eagle Crag
High Crag Butress
Comb Crags
Sheepbone Butress
Raven Crag
White Cove
Path
High Crag
744

5 **C** ***Harrow Buttress*** **(45m, Diff, W. Bishop & W.A. Woodsend, 1912)**

Starts in a small bay just left of lowest point of the crag.

P1 25m: Climb the book corner at the back of the bay to a ledge (good belay here if desired). Go up a clean chimney, traverse left for about 3m and climb to a ledge with a block belay.

P2 20m: Climb the groove above the belay and scramble over jumbled rocks to below an overhung corner. Go left of the corner, up to the ridge and follow this easily until the buttress peters out.

A rough path leads up the ridge over vegetation and stones then drops down into the gully on the right. Scramble up the gully to beneath clean slabs on its right side (in ascent).

Grey Crag.

6 **C** ***Slabs Ordinary* (60m, V Diff, H. Bishop & W.A. Woodsend, 1913)**

P1 20m: An obvious traverse line leads rightwards to a stepped crack-line that leads comfortably up and rightward to blocks. Surmount these blocks and pad up the left side of a large sloping ledge to belay at its further end.

P2 20m: Climb easy-angled rock above to a short crack and go up slabs to the foot of a right-facing corner and belay.

P3 20m: Climb the corner, which trends leftwards to finish on good holds to the top.

Oxford and Cambridge Buttress now comes into full view across a notch. Before scrambling down into the notch and across to the foot of the buttress, survey the potential routes. The classic *Oxford and Cambridge Direct* follows the main arête that rises directly ahead while the easier *Oxford and Cambridge Ordinary Route* takes a wandering line up the slabs on the left.

If time and inclination allow, the recommended tactic is to leave rucksacks at the foot of the buttress, climb the *Direct* unencumbered, descend the gully on the right (facing out) of the crag, don sacks and climb the *Ordinary* route.

Alex Reid begins pitch 2 of *Oxford and Cambridge Direct.*

Earlier, on pitch 1 of *Slabs Ordinary.*

7a **C** ***Oxford and Cambridge Direct*** **(40m, Severe, H.V. Reade, 1914)**

P1 **15m:** Start just right of the foot of the arête and soon work round to its left and pull on to the crest. Continue up to a ledge.

P2 **25m:** Move left and tackle the crux – a bulge with a challenging crack, protectable with a cam. Work right to the arête and follow this, surmounting another awkward bulge, to the top.

7b **C** ***Oxford and Cambridge Ordinary Route*** **(40m, Hard Diff, H.V. Reade, 1914)**

P1 **15m:** Start left of the arête and climb stepped rock to a ledge and belay.

P2 **10m:** Traverse left across the face to a corner beneath a bulging overhang: the crux. Pull over this on good holds and belay immediately above.

P3 **15m:** Continue pleasantly up the corner to the top.

8 The buttress climbs finish close to the High Stile summit cairn (807m). From here go south-west to a cairn on the main ridge of the massif and follow a path descending west, then swinging north-west, for 1.3km to Red Pike.

9 Red Pike (755m). From the summit cairn descend north-east on a ridge called the Saddle, a steep path on skittery red stones. After about 500m the path turns south-east and drops to Bleaberry Tarn.

10 From the tarn follow the path – now on white stones – north-east, winding increasingly steeply down the fellside, often on laid steps, down to trees at Old Burtness and on to rejoin the outward route at **Point 2.**

Chockstone Buttress, Grey Crag. Climbers on *Slabs Ordinary* (right) and *Slabs West Route* (left).

Finishing the *Lorton Gully* scramble, Grasmoor. Lanthwaite and Lorton vale below.

07 Lorton Gully Circuit 8km Grade 3

Puzzle and punishment in a gloriously greasy gully

LANTHWAITE – *Lorton Gully*, Grade 3 – **COLEDALE HAUSE** – **LIZA BECK** – **LANTHWAITE**

The day

The western flank of Grasmoor is one of the highest continuous steep slopes in the Lake District, sweeping 600 metres to the felltop. From here two gullies descend: both offer sport to the scrambler-climber and the most prominent of the two, *Lorton Gully*, is an adventurer's treat. In all but drought conditions, its deepest recesses demand techniques akin to aid climbing. Fortunately, the worst horrors can be bypassed.

Grasmoor is a bulwark of the western Lake District and looks out across the Solway estuary and the Irish Sea. It follows that the best time of day to tackle *Lorton Gully* is late afternoon when any sun might penetrate its interior. And ideal conditions would be a prolonged dry spell. However this is the Cumbrian coast and it is much more likely you will encounter pitches of incredibly greasy rock and need to start earlier in the day to complete the round – but a challenge is what *Lorton Gully* is about.

Though the line of the gully is in plain sight from the car park, it is hard to gauge what conditions might be like within. A rope and basic rack are therefore essential unless you are happy to turn the slipperiest pitches. The gully has a vertical height of some 450 metres and most of the difficulties occur in the lower third. The way then divides at a ten-metre-high wall, with an optional pitch at Severe; the gully becomes shallow with the best entertainment on the broken rocks to its left.

The climbing ends at a cairn on the lip of the fell, from where it is a stroll over the summit of grassy Grasmoor (852 metres) to Coledale Hause. An energetic finish would be to take in Hopegill Head (770 metres) and the fine ridge to Whiteside. However most will feel they've done enough for one day and descend by Liza Beck, pondering the possibilities of the broken ridges of Gasgale Crags or looking for dippers that frequent the heather-banked stream.

The second of the two gullies, *Buttermere Gully*, is tucked away to right. It is shorter and offers climbing up to Diff standard. Both gullies are marked on the OS 1:25000 map.

LORTON GULLY CIRCUIT

DISTANCE: 8km **TOTAL ASCENT:** 920m **START:** Lanthwaite Green GR: NY 159208
TIME: Dependent on conditions, 5–7.5hrs **CLIMBING:** None **SCRAMBLING:** *Lorton Gully*, 430m, Grade 3/optional Severe
MAP: OS Explorer OL4, The English Lakes North-western area, 1:25000
REFRESHMENTS: Kirkstile Inn, Loweswater (T: 01900 85219); cafés and pubs Buttermere

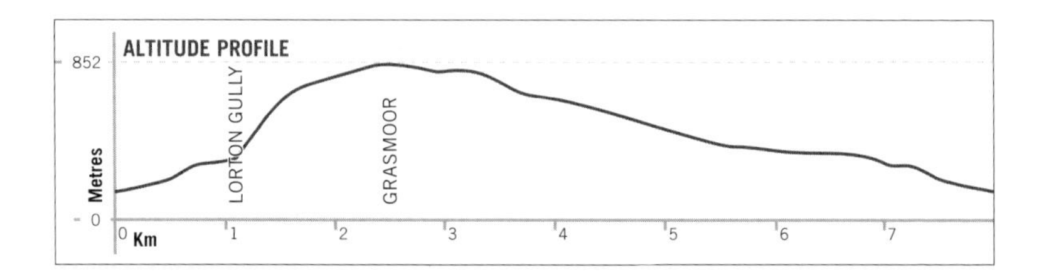

The Route **Lorton Gully Circuit**

Start

Lanthwaite, 5km north-west of Buttermere on the B5289. Car park with public telephone just south of Lanthwaite Green Farm. **GR: NY 159208.**

S From the Lanthwaite Green car park *Lorton Gully* is clearly visible, cleaving the flank of Grasmoor to the south-east. The best line of approach is to take a grassy path rising gently eastwards for five minutes, then branch right up a bracken-covered ridge that descends from the foot of Grasmoor.

2 When this steepens at 250m, (15 minutes from the car park) traverse right across the fellside to broken rocks with a rowan (mountain ash) tree at their foot. Cross scree and go over the bank to arrive in the amphitheatre at the foot of the gully.

ROUTE CONTINUES OVERLEAF

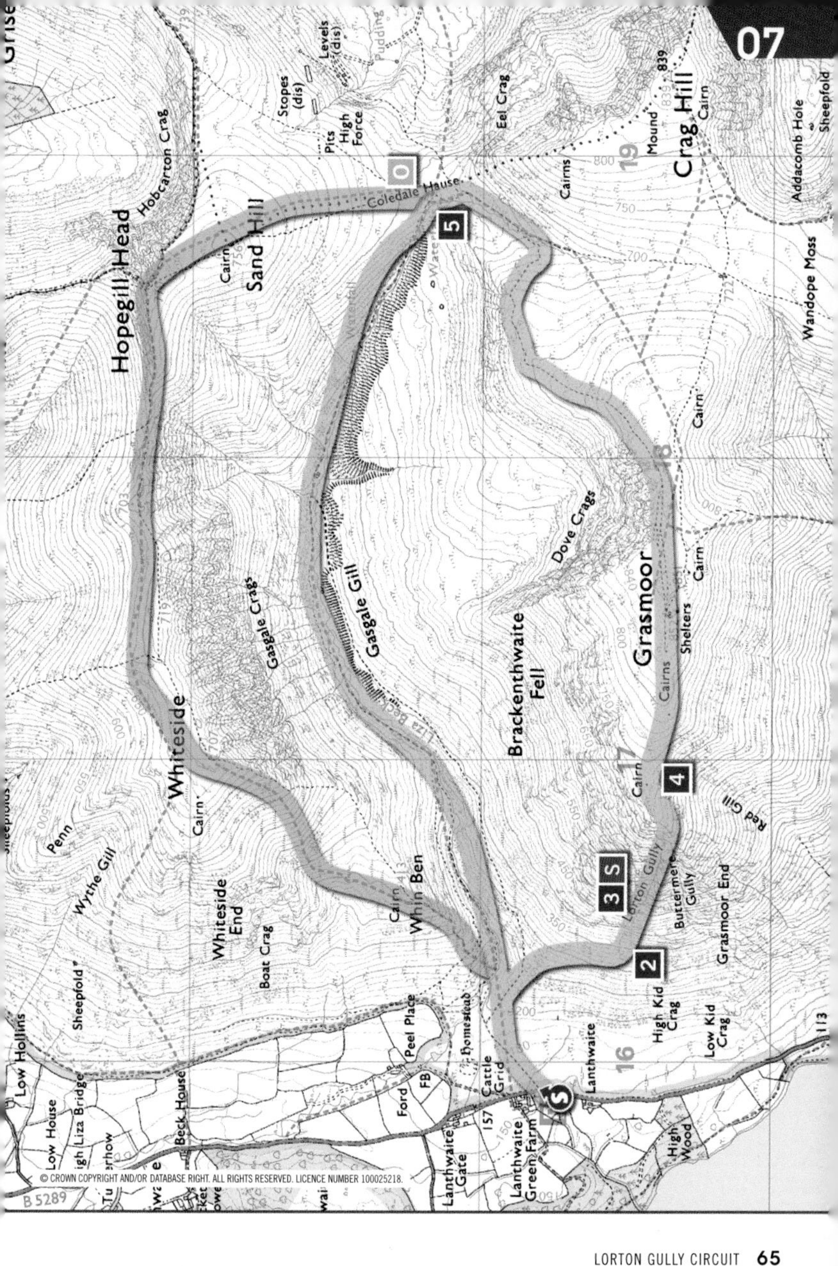

07
Hopegill Head
Hobcarton Crag
Sand Hill
Coledale Hause
Crag Hill
Eel Crag
Grasmoor
Dove Crags
Brackenthwaite Fell
Gasgale Gill
Gasgale Crags
Whiteside
Whiteside End
Whin Ben
Liza Beck
Lorton Gully
Buttermere Gully
Grasmoor End
High Kid Crag
Low Kid Crag
Lanthwaite
Lanthwaite Green Farm
Lanthwaite Gate
Cattle Grid
Peel Place
Beck House
Low Hollins
Low House
Liza Bridge
Wythe Gill
Penn
Boat Crag
Wandope Moss
Addacomb Hole
Red Gill
High Wood
B 5289

3 **S** ***Lorton Gully* (430m, Grade 3, FA pre 1894)**

The scramble begins over slabby rock steps and moves into a narrowing gash where the first slimy rock is likely to be encountered. If it's dry, this could be your lucky day. Otherwise you'll be getting damp and dirty chimneying up the steep exit – good holds to finish.

The streambed becomes easier angled, between heather and gorse, before entering a bay beneath a holly tree. The fissured rock on the right is pleasant when dry, but if it's wet the surest exit is at the very back, climbing up between the boughs of the holly – minus rucksack.

More heather wading leads to a dark slit which is the crux of the route. Within tight, greasy walls the gully rises in three increasingly difficult steps, each about 5m. The climber is drawn inexorably on as possibilities for placing protection diminish. If the gully is wet and the top of the final step mossy and running with water, an awkward retreat may be inevitable. Escape is from the foot of the slit, on heather to the left.

Above the crux, the gully enters an open bay at the 450m contour and divides at a wall with a reddish corner at its right end. For climbers happy to lead Severe this is the way to go, starting up the corner crack and finishing leftwards on the wall. Unfortunately, this too is often damp. The scrambler, meanwhile, has choices. The wall can be tackled at its more broken left end to re-enter the gully. However, from here upwards the most entertaining rock lies further left where steps, ledges, short walls and patches of heather can be linked according to taste, eventually joining the north-west ridge and a thin path.

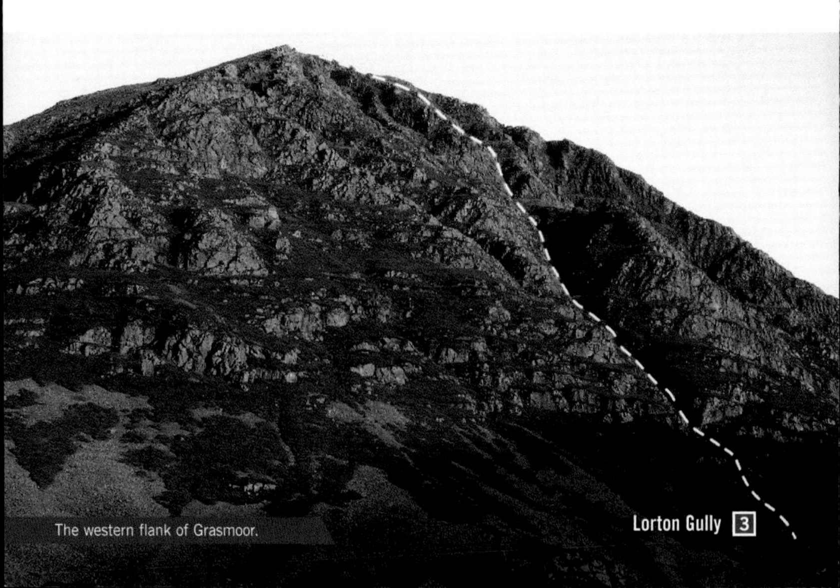

The western flank of Grasmoor.

4 From a cairn on the lip of the fell at 735m, easy walking leads eastwards to the summit windbreak on Grasmoor (852m). Descend to Coledale Hause, either by the main path or, more scenically, by a lesser path skirting the top of Dove Crags and the north slope of the mountain.

5 Coledale Hause (600m). Descend westwards beside cascades and follow the Liza Beck down Gasgale Gill for 3km to a footbridge. Cross the beck and breast a slight rise to rejoin the outward path to car park.

O Alternatively, from Coledale Hause the walk could be extended by continuing northward over Sand Hill (756m) to Hopegill Head (770m), then westwards along the ridge to Whiteside (719m), descending via Whin Ben (413m) to the footbridge (referred to in **Point 4**) over the Liza Beck. This would add about one hour to the circuit.

Lorton Gully: a hanging garden of greasy rock and plant life.

Sharp Edge: exhilarating scramble to Blencathra.

08 Bannerdale Crags & Sharp Edge Circuit

10km Grade 1

A classic scramble crowns a fine fell wander

SCALES (ON A66) – GLENDERAMACKIN VALLEY – BANNERDALE CRAGS – *Sharp Edge,* Grade 1 **– BLENCATHRA – HALL'S FELL RIDGE – SCALES**

The day

Sharp Edge is one of the two most popular scrambles in the Lake District, the other being *Striding Edge* on Helvellyn. And it's popular for good reason. Watch anyone reaching the top of the buttress that rises from the dorsal fin of the 'edge' to Atkinson Pike, and the smiling face says it all. Sometimes it may be tinged with relief, but always with a sense of satisfaction that comes from the full engagement of the senses in movement over rock in the high hills. *Sharp Edge* gives that buzz.

This Grade 1 scramble can be done in a short 'raid' of just a few hours from the roadside, but is better savoured as the main course in a longer, more varied, round. The route described here makes a fine day out with a light sack – no climbing gear needed – under the big skies of the wide-open northern fells.

From the A66 at Scales, our way skirts the eastern flank of Scales Fell then drops down to follow the River Glenderamackin downstream beneath a fell with the curious name of White Horse Bent. Did the name pass to the White Horse Inn at Scales? Vice versa? Leaving the river, we ascend Bannerdale Crags via the pronounced east ridge, winding through the remains of a nineteenth-century lead mine.

A broad view across the northern fells to the Solway Firth and hills of Galloway opens out as we stride from the bald plateau above the crags to the col at the head of the Glenderamackin.

Sharp Edge is now in full view, probably with scramblers silhouetted on its crest. Try not to feel pressured into rushing the ascent. Take a pleasure in choosing hand and footholds, and in your passage over and around the serrations of grey-green slate. Below your feet is Scales Tarn; it's said that on a windless day you can see the stars reflected in its dark waters.

At Blencathra's summit (868 metres), a new panorama is revealed, south across the Vale of Keswick to Derwentwater and the central fells. And dipping away at our feet is the mile-long Hall's Fell, a pleasing descent over rocky crusts and shale to a fell-foot path back to Scales. In August these southern flanks of Blencathra – or Saddleback – are bishop purple with heather.

BANNERDALE CRAGS & SHARP EDGE CIRCUIT

DISTANCE: 10km **TOTAL ASCENT:** 955m **START:** Scales Green GR: NY 340268 **TIME:** 5hrs **CLIMBING:** None **SCRAMBLING:** *Sharp Edge*, 180m, Grade 1 **MAP:** OS Explorer OL5: The English Lakes North-eastern area, 1:25000 **REFRESHMENTS:** White Horse Inn, Scales (T: 017687 79883); Salutation (T: 017687 79614) and Horse & Farrier (T: 017687 79688), Threlkeld

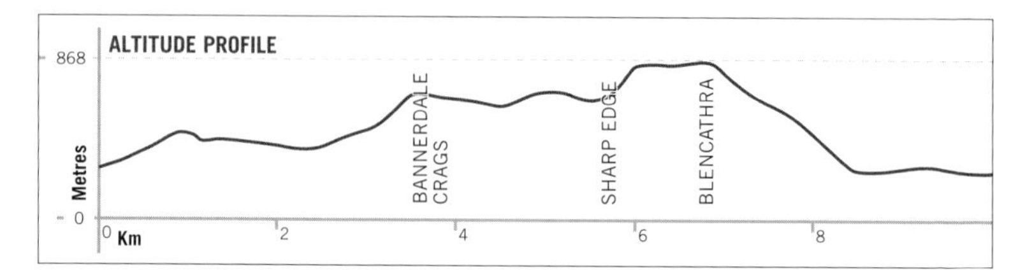

The Route

Bannerdale Crags & Sharp Edge Circuit

Start

Scales Green on the A66, 2km north-east of Threlkeld village and 300m west of the White Horse Inn. Layby parking. **GR: NY 340268.**

S From Scales Green a public footpath sign points between two cottages to where a kissing gate gives access to the fell. Go through the gate and bear right on a path between gorse bushes, curving up round the east flank of Scales Fell. At the junction, approximately 20 minutes from the start, continue straight over – **not** left directly up the fellside. The path soon rises steeply and then eases off to traverse above Mousthwaite Comb to a junction at the west end of the col that divides the comb and valley of River Glenderamackin.

2 Continue straight for 15m until a track on the far bank of the Glenderamackin comes into view. Make a bee-line down the grassy slope until a wooden bridge comes into view and aim for this.

3 Cross the bridge and follow a good track down the valley. After 10 minutes' easy strolling, Bannerdale Ridge comes into view, descending from the craggy skyline on the left. The ascent route can be seen angling up on the opposite side of the stream that drains the cwm, heading towards mine debris.

ROUTE CONTINUES OVERLEAF

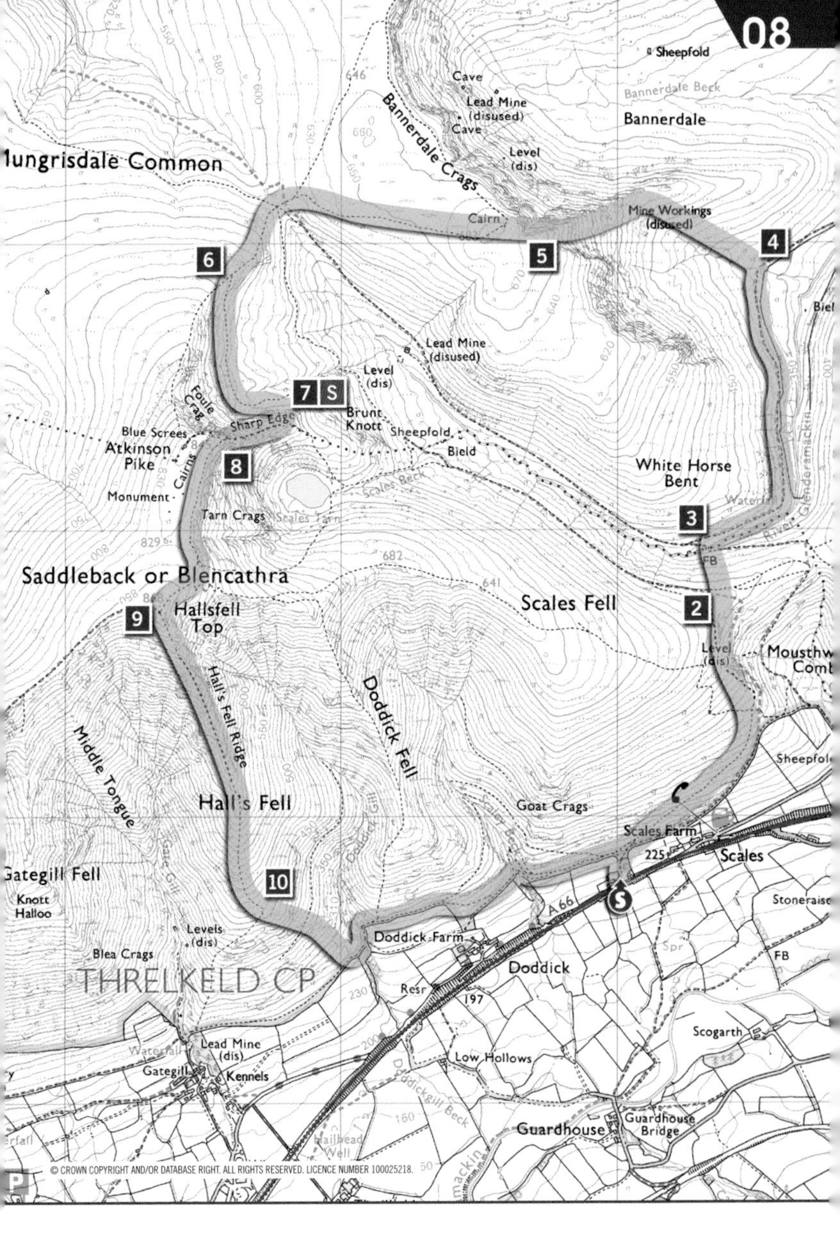
Sheepfold
Cave
Lead Mine
(disused)
Cave
Bannerdale Beck
Bannerdale
Bannerdale Crags
Level
(dis)
Mungrisdale Common
Cairn
Mine Workings
(disused)
4
5
6
Lead Mine
(disused)
Level
(dis)
7
S
Foule Crag
Sharp Edge
Brunt Knott
Sheepfold
Blue Screes
Atkinson Pike
Bield
8
Cairns
Monument
White Horse Bent
Scales Beck
Tarn Crags
Scales Tarn
3
River Glenderamackin
FB
Saddleback or Blencathra
Scales Fell
9
Hallsfell Top
2
Hall's Fell Ridge
Doddick Fell
Middle Tongue
Mousthwaite Comb
Sheepfold
Hall's Fell
Goat Crags
Scales Farm
Scales
Gategill Fell
10
A 66
Knott Halloo
Stoneraise
Levels
(dis)
Doddick Farm
Blea Crags
Doddick
FB
THRELKELD CP
Resr
Scogarth
Lead Mine
(dis)
Gategill
Kennels
Low Hollows
Doddickgill Beck
Guardhouse
Guardhouse Bridge
Hallhead Well

4 Just after fording the stream turn left on a grassy path up through bracken. Continue through spoil piles to Bannerdale Ridge. Turn uphill and follow the slate-strewn 'path' winding through old workings and steeply up the ridge. At the top, follow the lip of the crag rightwards to a slate cairn (681m) finely-positioned overlooking Bannerdale.

5 Head westward to the actual summit (683m), 50m away across the plateau, marked by a small heap of stones. Take a grassy path west-north-west to the col and the path junction at the head of the upper Glenderamackin. Ascend the main track towards Blencathra for about 10 minutes, looking left of the path for a tiny cairn (*c.*690m) that marks the way down into the valley.

6 Follow a faint trail curving beneath Foule Crag and then gradually up to the eastern end of the ridge topped by *Sharp Edge*. Leave the path and ascend directly up steep grass to the foot of the edge proper – joined by the main path coming up from Scales Tarn.

On *Sharp Edge*: popular, with good reason.

7 **S** ***Sharp Edge* (180m, Grade 1)**

Sharp Edge rises some 180m over a length of 350m. Keep as close as practicable to the crest for the best scrambling. Diversionary 'paths' worn on the north side can lead to difficulties. The rock is polished and can be slippery when wet.

The scramble changes character at the notch that separates the 'dorsal' part of the ridge from the blunter buttress. Pick a line to suit your climbing taste; the easiest is up a shallow trench that provides a rough stair ascending from the west side of the notch.

8 At the top, turn south along the rim of Tarn Crags, soon swinging west to Blencathra summit (868m).

9 *Hall's Fell Ridge* descends south-south-east directly from the summit. Easier than *Sharp Edge*, it still demands care. Below about 500m the ridge broadens and a low cairn is reached. At a second cairn on a brow, turn left on a faint track over grass, heading east. (The main path swings right for Threlkeld.)

10 Descend steeply south-east to join a path along the foot of the fells. Turn left to cross Doddick Gill and continue east to Scaley Beck. (The descent to the beck gives a last, brief opportunity to set hands to rock.) Follow the path, beneath larches, to the kissing gate at the start.

Sharp Edge from the approach path above Scales Tarn.

2

Langdale & Ullswater

Langdale is perhaps the most popular of Lakeland valleys, and after a day tackling routes featured here on Pavey Ark or Bowfell Buttress, you may well think justly so. For solitude, head over to Ullswater and try Hutaple Crag and Greenhow End above Deepdale, or visit the quiet Greenburn valley, beyond Little Langdale, for a scramble up Wetherlam.

Wild weather on *Pinnacle Ridge* (climber Jo Campbell).

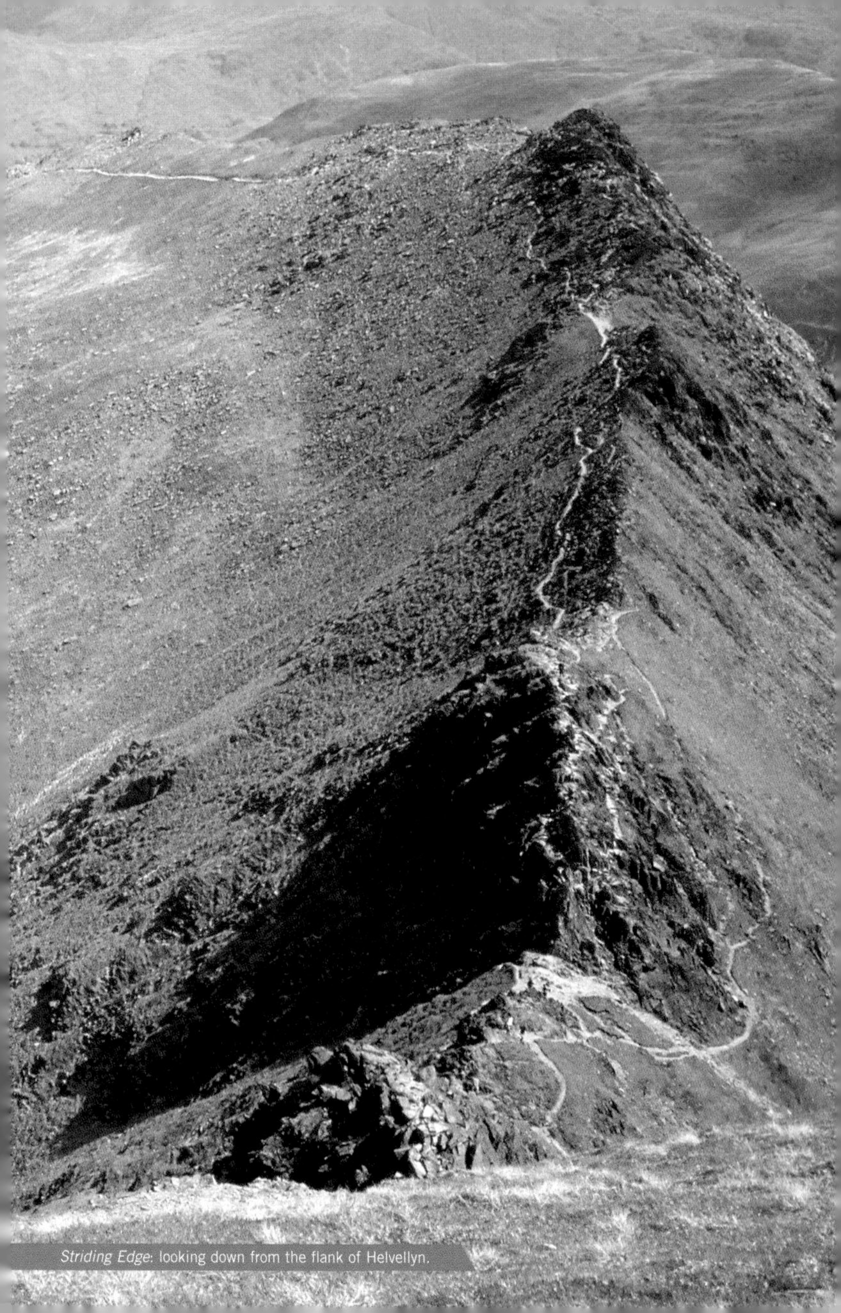

Striding Edge: looking down from the flank of Helvellyn.

09 Pinnacle Ridge & Striding Edge

16km Mod/Diff

Cracks, pinnacles and a stride on a celebrated skyline

PATTERDALE – GRISEDALE – *Pinnacle Ridge,* Mod/Diff **– ST SUNDAY CRAG – GRISEDALE TARN – DOLLYWAGGON PIKE – HELVELLYN –** *Striding Edge,* Grade 1 **– GRISEDALE – PATTERDALE**

The day

Pinnacle Ridge is arguably the best scramble in the Lake District. This, of course, is a subjective assertion. Weather, the state of the rock, companions or simply one's mood on the day will colour any judgement. But I'm sticking to it.

Clean rock for pitched climbing and scrambling is less abundant on these eastern fells than in the central Lakes. It also takes more searching out, with the exception of the justifiably popular *Striding Edge* that forms the homeward leg of this round.

Situated on the north-western flank of St Sunday Crag overlooking Grisedale, *Pinnacle Ridge* is a top-grade scramble with one short pitch of climbing touching Diff. This poses the question of whether to take a rope or not. Traditionally the ridge was soloed, but nowadays most parties rope up. That's certainly wise if any of the party is inexperienced or if there is a likelihood of the rock being wet; there is a fair degree of exposure.

Although the ridge is undoubtedly pinnacled, these features are not obvious from below and if none of the party has been on the ridge before, locating the foot of the route can cause some head-scratching. Once engaged though, the scramble is a delight, surmounting slabs and jumbled blocks before entering a deep corner where fissures at the back form the crux of the route. For most, it proves less daunting than on first sight, with good handholds just when required.

Regaining the ridge for an airy crossing of the final pinnacle you'll be wishing the route was twice as long. However the day is far from over. A short walk gains the summit of St Sunday Crag. Then comes the descent to Grisedale Tarn followed by a steady climb over Dollywaggon and Nethermost pikes and on to Helvellyn – at 950 metres the third highest peak in the Lake District.

Striding Edge may barely rate as a Grade 1 scramble, but it has an enduring appeal, and a quality of form best appreciated in descent, as proposed here. As you stand on the lip of the plateau, the ridge drops away steeply at first and then levels out to a rocky spine, poised between the cold eye of Red Tarn and the wild emptiness of Nethermost Cove. It's the total situation for the scrambler – sticking as closely to the crest as prudent and moving fluidly up and down a succession of polished rock steps – that makes *Striding Edge* a joy; a perfect complement to the more technical challenge of *Pinnacle Ridge.*

PINNACLE RIDGE & STRIDING EDGE

DISTANCE: 16km **TOTAL ASCENT:** 1,150m **START:** Grisedale Bridge GR: NY 391162 **TIME:** 8hrs **CLIMBING:** None **SCRAMBLING:** *Pinnacle Ridge*, 140m, Mod/Diff, or Grade 2 if crux is bypassed; *Striding Edge*, in descent -130m, Grade 1 **MAP:** OS Explorer OL5: The English Lakes North-eastern area, 1:25000 **REFRESHMENTS:** Two pubs in Patterdale, pubs and cafés in Glenridding

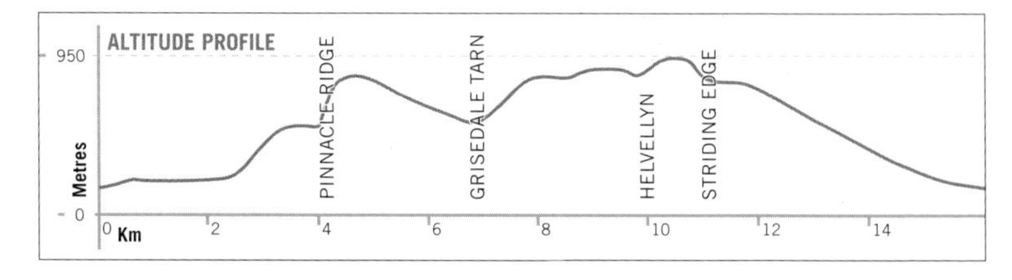

The Route
Pinnacle Ridge & Striding Edge

Start

Grisedale Bridge on the A592, just west of Patterdale parish church. The nearest car park is opposite the Patterdale Hotel, with two large car parks at Glenridding, 1km north. **GR: NY 391162.**

S From Grisedale Bridge, follow the tarmac lane south-west up Grisedale.

2 After 1km, where the public road turns sharp right, continue straight ahead on a farm track, keeping the beck away to your right and eventually passing a house and farm buildings at Elmhow.

3 At the north-west corner of Elmhow Plantation go through the gate and turn left, off the main track and uphill, picking up a grassy path that leads round the south-west corner of the plantation, fords a small stream, then zigzags up the fellside towards Blind Cove and the skyline.

4 At *c*.470m the gradient eases to almost a shelf below Blind Cove. Leave the path here – before it swings leftwards – and traverse south-west across the fellside, aiming for below the broken crags of St Sunday. An indistinct path leads across boggy ground towards rocks and scree. If you lose the path, as is quite likely, continue to skirt the foot of the crags. Cross two minor scree chutes to a larger one descending well down the fellside. *Pinnacle Ridge* should now be above you. Zigzag upwards.

Helvellyn
Catstye Cam
Red Tarn
Striding Edge
Swirral Edge
Hole-in-the-Wall
Nethermost Pike
Dollywaggon Pike
High Crag
Grisedale Tarn
Grisedale Forest
Patterdale Common
St Sunday Crag
Pinnacle Ridge
Deepdale Common
PATTERDALE CP
Deepdale Hause
Birks
Grisedale
Grisedale Brow
Deepdale
Hartsop above How
Brothers' Parting Stone
Willie Wife Moor
Birk Side
© CROWN COPYRIGHT AND/OR DATABASE RIGHT. ALL RIGHTS RESERVED. LICENCE NUMBER 100025218.

5 **C** ***Pinnacle Ridge*** **(140m, Mod/Diff, G.A. Leaver, Miss S.A. Evans, B.W. Lowthian, M.E. Twentyman, 1955)**

A low cairn on the left side of a gully (looking up) marks the start of the route. A rowan tree is just visible high on the right side of the ridge, overlooking the gully.

Ascend the ridge on spiky blocks, keeping close to the gully lip at first for the best scrambling. The popularity of the ridge as a winter climb means the route is increasingly 'signposted' by crampon scratches. Moving rightwards, ascend towards a 'gun barrel' atop a smooth slab and projecting out over Grisedale. Turn the slab by slipping behind a block on its right.

Easier ground leads to the foot of a steep buttress. Scramble round the left side of this and into a damp corner with vertical cracks at the back, right of a steep wall. This is the crux but can be protected with nuts or cams. The first couple of moves, getting established in the groove, are the trickiest, after which adequate handholds materialise.

Grisedale and Ullswater viewed from *Pinnacle Ridge*.

Note: *If, for whatever reason, you don't like the look of this pitch, it can be avoided via the grubby gully left of the steep wall. Descend slightly to enter the gully, scramble up its left side and traverse back across to rejoin the route on ledges above the crux. This option turns the route into a Grade 2 scramble.*

Move left over ledges at the top of the groove and climb fissures in a steep step and on up further ledges to a superb spiny crest. There is considerable exposure here, underlined when you top out on the pinnacle and realise a steep descent must be made to a notch. Small edges provide sufficient footholds, but tread carefully.

Scramble out of the notch to a shale slope and up to a concluding climb over steep blocks.

Clean rock and generous holds on *Pinnacle Ridge*.

6 From the top of *Pinnacle Ridge*, walk up to the summit of St Sunday Crag, some 400m southwards.

7 From the summit cairn(s) on St Sunday Crag (841m), follow the path south-west down a broad ridge.

8 At Deepdale Hause (*c.*700m) a path forks right towards Grisedale. Follow this, descending steeply at first, then traversing more gently to Grisedale Tarn.

9 At the tarn cross the outflow stream and ascend a good path up the southern flank of Dollywaggon Pike. The path leads over High Crag and Nethermost Pike to Helvellyn (1 hour 15 minutes from the tarn).

10 Helvellyn (950m). From the summit windbreak, walk a short distance south-east past the memorial to Charles Gough and his faithful dog to the lip of the plateau. *Striding Edge* stretches out eastwards below your feet, with Red Tarn on its north side. (Gough perished here in 1805 and his dog stayed by his side for three months.)

11 **S** ***Striding Edge* (in descent, -130m, Grade 1)**

The descent is steep and skittery at first, down to a notch where the 'edge' abuts the bulk of the mountain. A short scramble up polished rock – several variants – gains the crest of the ridge. Adhere to this until the scrambling peters out.

The path descends to a junction at the Hole-in-the-Wall (710m).

12 Cross the ladder-stile to the south-east side of the wall and follow the path angling down east into Grisedale for 2km to Brownend Plantation.

13 By larches, turn right through the gate and go straight down the grass field to a tarmac lane. Follow this south-south-east over Grisedale Beck and rejoin the outward route to return to Patterdale.

Jo Campbell on the crest of *Pinnacle Ridge*.

Greenhow End at the head of Deepdale.

10 Greenhow End & Hutaple Crag

12km Diff

Climbing or scrambling on routes less trodden in wild Deepdale

DEEPDALE BRIDGE – DEEPDALE – GREENHOW END (*Greenhow End*, Grade 1**) OR HUTAPLE CRAG (***Far West Rib, Western Avenue*, Diff**) – FAIRFIELD – HART CRAG – HARTSOP ABOVE HOW – DEEPDALE BRIDGE**

The day

Deepdale is a place of solitude and unfolding interest. Two valleys north, Glenridding is busy with folk treading the Red Tarn path to Helvellyn, and neighbouring Grisedale will also have modest traffic, but Deepdale … well, you will quite likely have it to yourself.

Perhaps we can thank William Wordsworth for Deepdale's tranquillity. The poet painted rather a grim picture of it in his 1810 *Guide to the Lakes*, declaring that the character of the valley 'may be conjectured from its name. It is terminated by a cove, a craggy and gloomy abyss, with precipitous sides; a faithful receptacle of the snows that are driven into it, by the west wind from the summit of Fairfield.'

Snow certainly does linger at the head of Deepdale, and those 'precipitous sides' probably provide the climbing and scrambling featured here. But 'gloomy' seems to me to be in the mind of the beholder. While the wanderer might indulge in certain melancholy in Deepdale's wild recesses, for the climber there is the satisfaction of picking a line up seldom-travelled ground.

High in Deepdale are two crags well regarded (though little visited) by rock climbers – Scrubby Crag above Link Cove and Hutaple Crag above Sleet Cove.

Between the two lies the bulky promontory of Greenhow End. This is where we're bound, either for an easy scramble up the nose of Greenhow End or for a climb on Hutaple Crag.

Both routes come together on the brow of the promontory and from there it is a felltop day, visiting the bald top of Fairfield (873 metres) and Hart Crag (822 metres) before returning over Hartsop above How (580 metres) with a fine view over Deepdale and to the far eastern fells. This last is really just a rise on a long ridge, sweeping north-east from Hart Crag for three enjoyable kilometres before it drops through parkland with old thorn trees and ashes towards Deepdale Bridge.

If you opt for the Grade 1 scramble on Greenhow End then this is a light sack day. For the climb on Hutaple Crag, however, you will need rope, rack and a good eye for route finding. Hutaple is a big, broken crag of serious mien. Our ascent links two Diff grade routes at the western extremity of the crag: *Far West Rib* and *Western Avenue*. In 2013, neither showed any signs of recent passage and arranging belays was not straightforward – 'Diffs with attitude' was our verdict.

GREENHOW END & HUTAPLE CRAG

DISTANCE: 12km **TOTAL ASCENT:** *c.*880m **START:** Deepdale Bridge GR: NY 399144
TIME: 8hrs with climb, 6hrs with scramble **CLIMBING:** *Far West Rib* 50m, Diff; *Western Avenue* 55m, Diff
SCRAMBLING: *Greenhow End*, 125m, Grade 1 **MAP:** OS Explorer OL5: The English Lakes North-eastern area, 1:25000
REFRESHMENTS: Two pubs in Patterdale, pubs and cafés in Glenridding

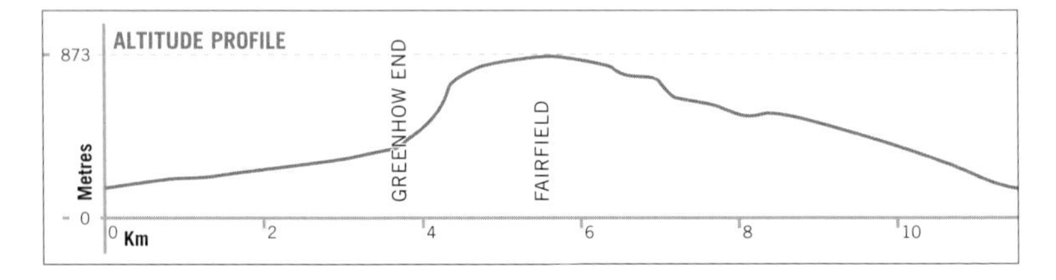

The Route

Greenhow End & Hutaple Crag

Start

Deepdale Bridge on the A592, 1.5km south of Patterdale village. Parking on south side of the bridge and in a layby north of houses. **GR: NY 399144.**

From Deepdale Bridge follow a minor lane westwards from the north side of the bridge for 400m to Lane Head. Turn left through a gate and continue past Deepdale Hall and Wall End farm into Deepdale.

2 Approximately 2km from Wall End the path bears right, away from the beck and on to a low, grassy moraine ridge, heading for Sleet Cove. **Here you have a choice: continue on this path if bound for the climbs on Hutaple Crag. The way to the Greenhow End scramble bears left, following the beck upstream towards Link Cove.**

0 **For Greenhow End**: From Point 2 an indistinct path crosses streams and marshy ground south-west to the foot of the lowest cascades of Link Cove Beck. The gill itself makes an enjoyable scramble at Grade 2 (with an optional exposed pitch of V Diff) after a prolonged dry spell. It also provides ice climbing at Grade III in a deep freeze. Unfortunately both these circumstances are rare.

Assuming the gill is out of condition, follow the true left bank (right-hand looking up) of the beck to just above the last cascades where the slope of the ground eases, then turn right (west) and cross the floor of the cove on about the 500m contour to the cliffs opposite.

Bridgend
Deepdale Bridge
Lane Head
Deepdale Hall
Aiken Crag
Trough Head
Birks
Cold Cove
Gavel Moss
Gavel Pike
Lord's Seat
Blind Cove
Pinnacle Ridge
St Sunday Crag
East Chockstone Gully
Y Gully
West Chockstone Gully
The Cape
Bannerside
Deepdale Common
PATTERDALE CP
Latterhaw Crag
Deepdale
Wall End
Sheepfold
Cockley How
Deepdale Park
Low Wood
Cow Bridge
Brothers Water
Sykeside
Caudalebeck Farm
Kirkstone Beck
Hartsop Dodd
Cora Crag
Wood Side
Bleaberry Knott
Gale Crag
Hoggill Brow
Buck Stones
The Perch
Gill Crag
Hartsop above How
Stony Rigg
Holly Crag
Black Crag
Blake Brow
Erne Nest Crag
Mossydale
Isa Crag
Mart Crag
Greenhow End
Link Cove
The Step
Hutaple Crag
Hart Crag
Houndshope Cove
Shelter
Scrubby Crag
Black Tippet
Hog Ho
Black Buttress
Link Hause
Pile of Stones
Rydal Head
Flinty Grave
Fairfield
Fairfield Brow
Cofa Pike
Deepdale Hause
Cawk Cove
Sleet Cove
Grey Crag
Ruthwaite Lodge (Climbing Hut)
Dovedale
Thin Side
Bull Crag
Stangs
Nettle Cove
2
3
0
S
4–5
C
6
7
8

O S *Greenhow End* **(125m, Grade 1)**

Start on slabs *c.*15m left of a grass rake that rises rightwards. The rake forms a little-used walkers' route that zigzags to the top, twice intersecting the scramble. The cliff is very broken, alternating rock steps and slabs with grassy shelves. On first reaching the walkers' route cross rightwards to a rib. Continue searching out little problems and finish at a heap of stones on a flat rock on the nose of the crag.

Greenhow End.

Rock sculpture, Hart Crag.

On *Western Avenue* (climber Dave Hellier).

Hutaple Crag above Sleet Cove … 'a faithful receptacle of the snows', said Wordsworth.

3 **For Hutaple Crag:** follow Sleet Cove path for another 20 minutes, then bear off left, crossing the beck below the waterfalls (*c*.350m); ascend grassy slopes and traverse below the crag to its western end. Our two routes lie to the right of West Hutaple Gully (see topo opposite).

4 **C** ***Far West Rib* (50m, Diff, G.B. Spenceley, A.H. Griffin, C.E. Arnison, 1954)**

Start 10m right of the foot of the gully, and slightly higher. A rib, somewhat vegetated lower down, rises from steep grass. The rock is compact with small horizontal edges but limited protection. The route ends on a grass shelf with a nut belay 6m back, behind a boulder.

Western Avenue starts *c*.60m higher and rightwards of the finish of *Far West Rib*.

5 **C** ***Western Avenue* (55m, Diff)**

Ascend the clean rock of a *c*.9m-high buttress then continue up the rib, moving left at a break to finish up a second tier.

6 The Hutaple climb and Greenhow End scramble converge on The Step, from where a faint path rises south-west to join the main felltop highway. Turn right for Fairfield.

7 Fairfield (873m). Take in the extensive panorama, then return south-east and continue onwards to Link Hause and Hart Crag.

8 Hart Crag (822m). The broad ridge descending towards Hartsop above How is steep at first with no obvious path leading direct from the summit cairn. In mist there is a risk of striding off in the wrong direction. Coming from Link Hause, a rough path branches left off the main path before reaching the summit of Hart Crag and descends to the ridge. But if you continue to the summit it is necessary either to retrace your steps to this junction or to walk north-east until, after a short distance, the path is joined and the long ridge comes into view.

After the initial rocky descent, the ridge is very easy going, soft and boggy in places, the path maintaining a wonderfully elevated line for 3km before dropping down to a small plantation and across a grass field to Deepdale Bridge.

Water lilies on Easedale Tarn, skirted en-route to Belles Knott.

11 Belles Knott & Jack's Rake

16km Grade 1/2

Contrasting scrambles on a long felltop day

GRASMERE – **EASEDALE TARN** – *Belles Knott*, Grade 1 – **PAVEY ARK** (*Jack's Rake*, Grade 1/2) – **SERGEANT MAN** – **BLEA RIGG** – **SILVER HOW** – **GRASMERE**

The day

Alfred Wainwright described Belles Knott as the 'Matterhorn' of Easedale and depicted it so in pen and ink in one of his inimitable guidebooks. The Knott certainly looks impressive when approached, as here, from Easedale Tarn, and its skyline ridge provides entertaining scrambling on clean, rough rock. However, further comparison with the icon of Zermatt would be misplaced: there need be no pre-dawn start, no grumpy guides and no jostling crowds. Just you and an inquisitive raven perhaps.

Our second scramble of the day is likely to be busier. *Jack's Rake* is one of the most popular scrambles in Lakeland, part-trench, part-ledge, cutting diagonally across the massive face of Pavey Ark above Stickle Tarn.

At first glance, the linking of these two scrambles appears odd, Belles Knott being very much within the Grasmere orbit and Pavey Ark definitely a crag of Greater Langdale. In fact the two are barely an hour's walk apart, across the broad ridge between Sergeant Man and Blea Rigg and provide complementary, but wholly different, highlights in a long round of the central fells.

The day starts in bustling Grasmere – 'one more coffee for the road' is tempting – and follows the well-trodden track by Easedale Beck up to the eponymous tarn. If it has been dry for a few days, it's perfectly possible to step aside from the path and scramble up by the falls of Sourmilk Gill. The same is true of Easedale Gill, beside the path just below Belles Knott. Both gills offer Grade 1 scrambling, but each eats into your time, and you are going to need plenty; other parties could slow progress on *Jack's Rake* and the return leg over Sergeant Man and on to Silver How is long and taxing.

Three contrasting landscapes unfold: the picturesque Grasmere-Easedale side, becks tumbling between junipers, holly and rowans; the seemingly sheer rockscape of Pavey Ark – the biggest crag in crag-rich Langdale – reflected in Stickle Tarn (that is if the water is not being whipped by a westerly); and the undulating moor stretching three kilometres from Blea Rigg to Silver How, a somewhat disconcerting upland that feels strangely remote, though the busy Langdale valley lies, hidden mostly, just over the southern brow.

Most of the teashops will be closed by the time you get back to Grasmere, but if you've completed this whole circuit you'll probably be thirsting for something longer and stronger.

Grasmere Com
High Raise
High White Stones
762 Cairn
Stone
CP Bdy
Ash Crags
Deep Slack
Codale Head
Ferngill Crag
Deer Bields
Tarn Crag
Lang Crag
Codale Tarn
Slapestone Edge
Sergeant Man
Pile of Stones
Belles Knott
Bright Beck
Eagle Crag
Blea Crag
Blea Rigg
Pile of Stones
Thunacar Knott
Cairn
Path
Easy Gully
Pavey Ark
Harrison Stickle
Dam
Tarn Crag
Broad Crag
Langdale Pikes
Loft Crag
Thorn Crag
Whitegill Crag
Swine Knott
Scout Crag
Waterfalls
Gimmer Crag
Dungeon Ghyll
Pike Howe
Miller Crag
Stickle Ghyll
Green Howe
Raw Head
Dungeon Ghyll Force
Mark Gate
FB
Millbeck
New Hotel
Long House
White Crag
Waterfall
Raven Crag
FB
Rossett
Kirk Howe
Sheepfold
Middle Fell Farm
Rossett Bridge
Side House
Cumbria Way
Ford
B 5343
Stool End
Bield
Oak Howe Needle
Wall End
11
10
7
9
8
S
5–6
12

A stony road: Jeremy Laurance on the path by Easedale Gill.

Belles Knott rises above the optional scramble up Easedale Gill.

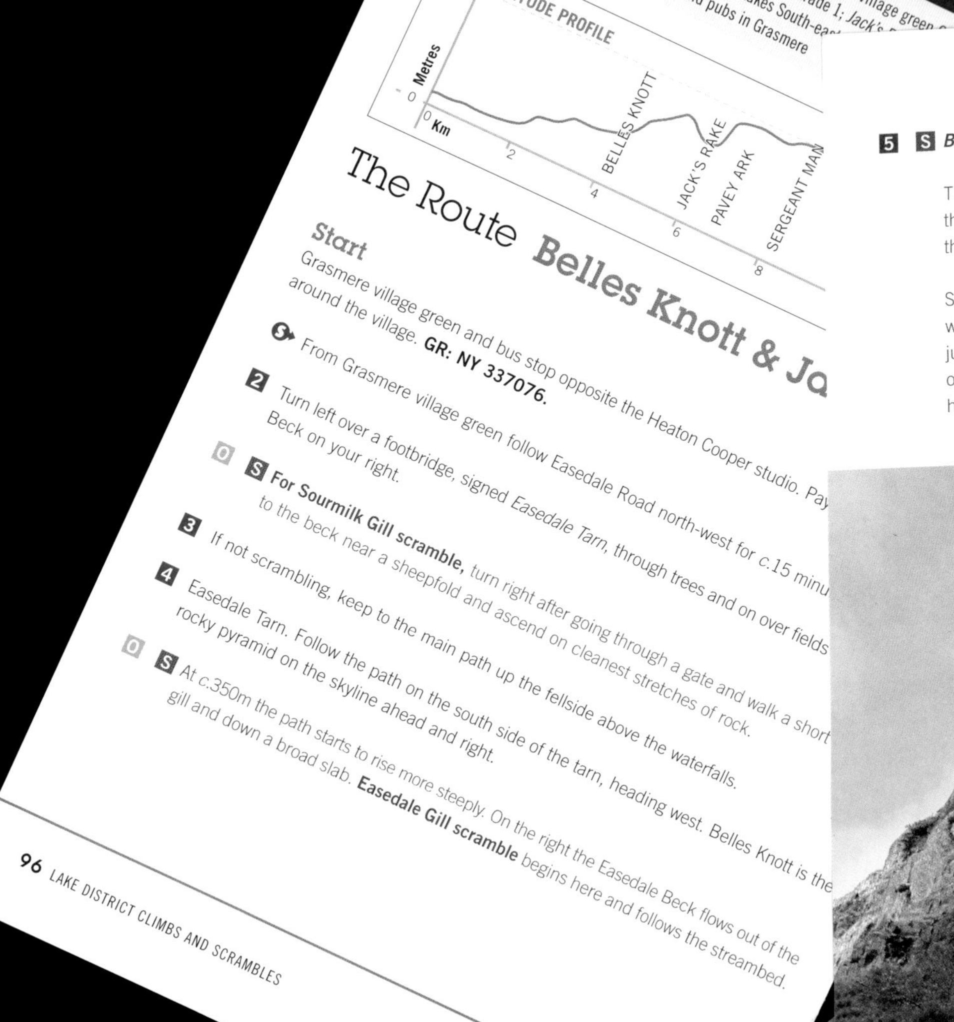

The Route Belles Knott & Ja...

Start

Grasmere village green and bus stop opposite the Heaton Cooper studio. Pay... around the village. **GR: NY 337076.**

From Grasmere village green follow Easedale Road north-west for c.15 minu...

2 Turn left over a footbridge, signed *Easedale Tarn*, through trees and on over fields... Beck on your right.

0 S **For Sourmilk Gill scramble,** turn right after going through a gate and walk a short... to the beck near a sheepfold and ascend on cleanest stretches of rock.

3 If not scrambling, keep to the main path up the fellside above the waterfalls.

4 Easedale Tarn. Follow the path on the south side of the tarn, heading west. Belles Knott is the... rocky pyramid on the skyline ahead and right.

0 S At c.350m the path starts to rise more steeply. On the right the Easedale Beck flows out of the gill and down a broad slab. **Easedale Gill scramble** begins here and follows the streambed.

5 S *Belles Knott* (50m, Grade 1)

The scramble begins at the foot of rocks that descend towards you when looking up from the path – to the right of what appears a steep south face. If not ascending Easedale Gill, the quickest approach is to continue on the path and cross the beck higher up.

Several tiny outcrops dot the fellside. Aim for where the rock appears most continuous, which should bring you to the start of the scramble at *c.*450m between a hawthorn and a juniper. Pull up a short wall left of the juniper and traverse right on a ramp behind the bush onto clean rock. A traverse left for 5m leads to the skyline arête, which is followed on good holds to the summit.

Belles Knott.

6 Belles Knott (*c.*510m). From the summit, walk north-west down the grassy hillside towards Codale Tarn. Follow the path south-west from the tarn to cross the beck and rejoin the main path ascending from Easedale. Continue up to the watershed.

7 Several paths converge on the ridge (*c.*600m) with a confusion of cairns. The simplest course is to continue ahead until Stickle Tarn and the south-facing cliff of Pavey Ark come into view, and then pick a line south-east down the steep bank to cross Bright Beck opposite where the path descends from Pavey. Cross Bright Beck at *c.*500m and contour round the hillside towards the foot of Pavey cliffs. With luck you will pick up an indistinct path that leads above the worst of the scree to join a well-worn zigzag up to the foot of *Jack's Rake*, just beyond the foot of *Easy Gully* which angles down from the right.

Entering Easedale Gill.

The author on the skyline of Belles Knott.

8 **S** ***Jack's Rake*** **(160m, Grade 1/2)**

The scramble follows a trough rising diagonally across Pavey's massive south face. There are no route-finding difficulties, but the rock is polished and can be slippery when wet (which is quite often since the trough is a natural drainage line). Drier rock can often be found on the stepped outer rim of the trough, but this is more exposed.

At about half height, the way levels out for a short stretch, passing the foot of *Gwynne's Chimney* (Diff) and the top of *The Crescent* (Diff) – both feature in **Route 12**. The *Rake* steepens again and eventually swings right, to bulging slabs. As is obvious, these have been climbed by several variations, all easy once the initial step up is made.

The route is now away from the cliff edge and scrambling up towards the ridge top. Before reaching the stone wall climb up rightwards over clean, rough rock, finishing close to the summit cairn.

Pavey Ark.

9 Pavey Ark (700m). From the cairn walk north-west over partly boggy ground to pick up the path that then swings northwards heading for High Raise.

10 At a broad col above the headwaters of Bright Beck, bear away from the High Raise path and instead take an indistinct path swinging eastwards and rising to Sergeant Man.

11 Sergeant Man (730m). Continue eastwards to a rocky knoll, descend to the path junction encountered earlier at **Point 7** and keep straight on, south-east. The path generally keeps to the highest ground; the peat hags before Blea Rigg are best skirted on the right.

12 Blea Rigg (541m). Fine view westwards to Langdale Pikes. Continue winding roughly south-east for 3km to Silver How, passing Swinescar Pike and to the north of the small tarns nestling on the plateau.

13 Silver How (394m). The last vantage point of the day, looking over the Vale of Grasmere. Take care getting the right descent route; while Grasmere lies north-east you must first go north-west and cross a beck in a gully; then northward through a tangle of magical junipers and finally north-east to Easedale Road.

Jack's Rake: an exposed stair slanting across the face of Pavey Ark.

Pavey Ark: *Crescent Climb* takes its name from the dipping traverse line in the centre of this photo, an exposed line above the slabs on the lower part of the face.

12 **Pavey Ark Circuit** 5km Mod/Diff

A Langdale enchaînement

GREAT LANGDALE, OLD DUNGEON GHYLL – *Middlefell Buttress*, Diff – **PAVEY ARK** (*Crescent Climb*, Mod – *Gwynne's Chimney*, Diff) – **HARRISON STICKLE** – **OLD DUNGEON GHYLL**

The day

From the valley bottom by the Old Dungeon Ghyll Hotel to the rock summit of Pavey Ark, this is an outing that keeps the mind of the climber-scrambler busy all the way. Its three multi-pitch climbs are each of different character – a clean buttress with a comfortable valley ambiance, a traverse line on a high mountain cliff where the sense of exposure belies its so-called 'moderate' grade, and an archetypal thrutchy chimney that gives way to open climbing virtually to the summit.

Great Langdale is justifiably popular, both with rock climbers and walkers. *Middlefell Buttress* (76 metres, Diff), the first of our routes for the day, has provided sport for countless novice climbers since its first ascent in 1911 – by a trio that included the Lake District pioneer Siegfried Herford – and its holds are unsettlingly polished as a consequence.

The buttress is often climbed on the approach to Gimmer Crag, higher to the north-west, but today we're heading north across the fellside towards Stickle Tarn and the imposing cliff that rises on its far side. At first sight, the line of *Crescent Climb* (100 metres, Mod) looks pretty daunting – 'Does it really traverse across the top of that steep slab?' Yes, it does, but by the time you've reached the foot of the arête the angle seems less intimidating.

Crescent Climb deposits you on *Jack's Rake*, an improbable ramp that slants diagonally up the cliff from right to left and is one of the Lake District's most popular scrambles (see Route 11). The choices are now between *Gwynne's Chimney* (24 metres, Diff), which begins just a few steps right of the finish of *Crescent*, an ascent of the *Rake* to the top of the crag, or a descent of the *Rake* for an early return to the valley. Factors to weigh are how wet the chimney looks and how much of the day remains.

All three Pavey routes have a long pedigree: *Jack's Rake* is the oldest recorded climb in the FRCC's *Langdale* guide, dating from the 1870s, though shepherds were probably using it much earlier; H.A. Gwynne gave his name to the *Chimney* in 1892 and *Crescent Climb* dates from 1907. It follows that all can be climbed in boots, as can *Middlefell Buttress*, though rock shoes are advisable if you attempt the direct start, graded Severe.

From the top of Pavey Ark (700 metres) the shortest descent is to scramble down *Jack's Rake*. However, our route continues over to Harrison Stickle (736 metres) and its magnificent vista of southern Lakeland. Either way, the bar at the Old Dungeon Ghyll makes an agreeable end to an energetic day.

PAVEY ARK CIRCUIT

DISTANCE: 5km **TOTAL ASCENT:** *c.*700m **START:** Old Dungeon Ghyll GR: NY 286061
TIME: Allow 8hrs **CLIMBING:** *Middlefell Buttress, Crescent Climb, Gwynne's Chimney* total c.300m, Diff
SCRAMBLING: Depends when rope is removed above *Gwynne's Chimney* and how much use is made of *Jack's Rake* – max 300m at Grade 1/2 **MAP:** OS Explorer OL6: The English Lakes South-western area, 1:25000
REFRESHMENTS: In Great Langdale: Old Dungeon Ghyll Hotel (T: 015394 37272); Sticklebarn Tavern (T: 015394 37356); and New Dungeon Ghyll Hotel (T: 015394 37213)

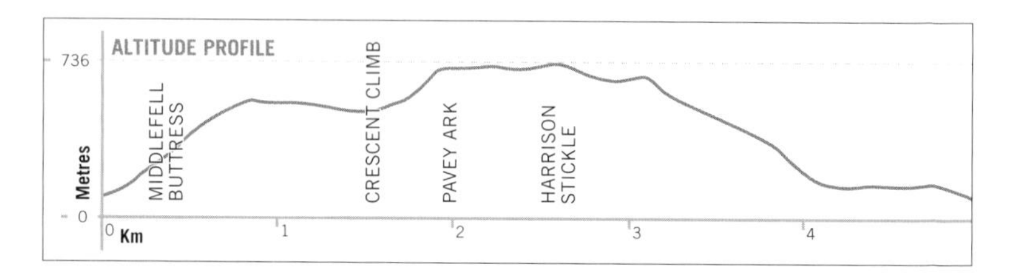

The Route **Pavey Ark Circuit**

Start

Old Dungeon Ghyll Hotel. Parking is available in the National Trust car park by the hotel at the head of Great Langdale (usually busy – more parking near the New Dungeon Ghyll). There is also a bus stop: service from Ambleside. **GR: NY 286061.**

Take the path behind the ODG, go through a gate and bear right up through a larch spinney and zigzag uphill on a stepped path towards Raven Crag. *Middlefell Buttress* is at the left end of the crag. Fork left to this, aiming for the foot of the buttress, right of a fence.

ROUTE CONTINUES OVERLEAF

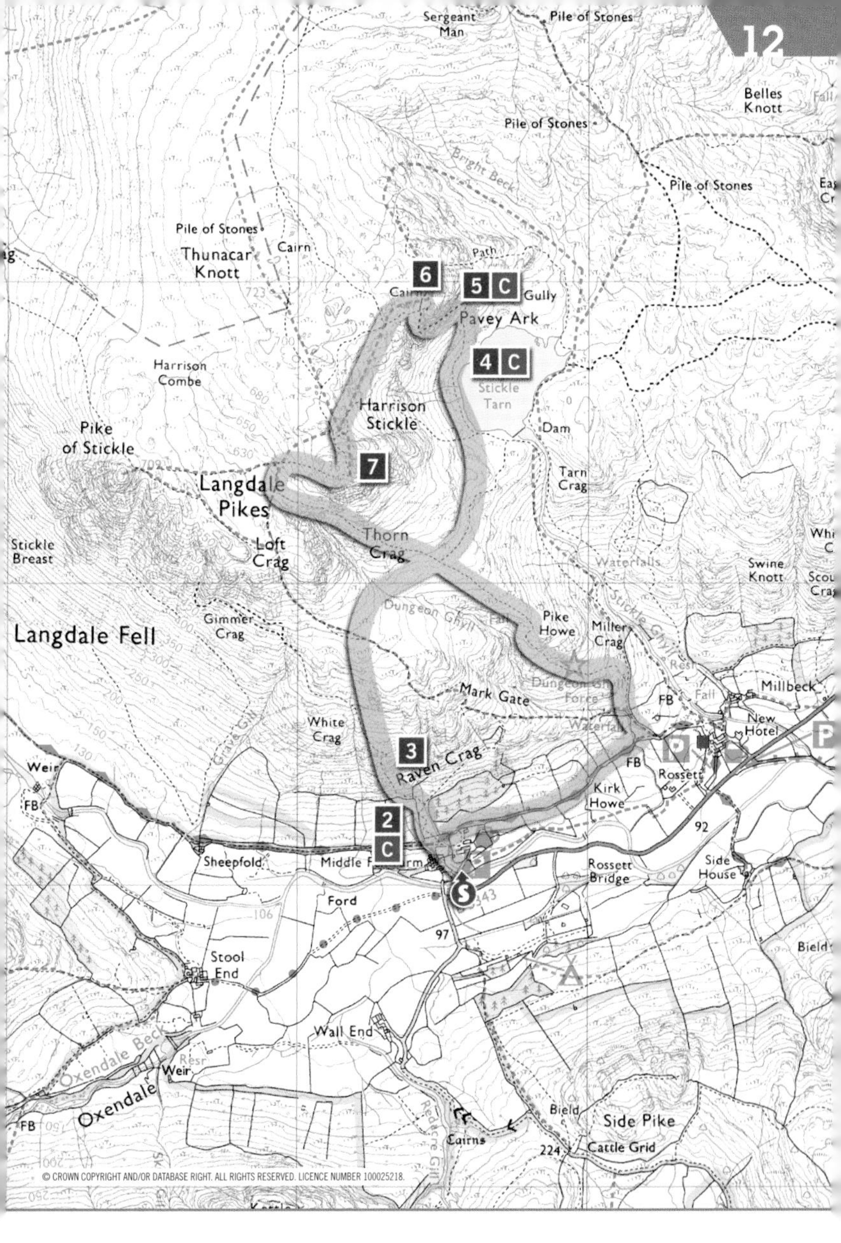
Sergeant Man
Pile of Stones
Belles Knott
Pile of Stones
Bright Beck
Pile of Stones
Pile of Stones
Thunacar Knott
Cairn
Path
6
Cairn
5 C
Gully
Pavey Ark
723
700
4 C
Stickle Tarn
Harrison Combe
680
Harrison Stickle
650
Dam
Pike of Stickle
630
7
709
Tarn Crag
Langdale Pikes
Thorn Crag
Stickle Breast
Loft Crag
Waterfalls
Swine Knott
Dungeon Ghyll
Stickle Ghyll
Gimmer Crag
Pike Howe
Miller Crag
Langdale Fell
350
300
250
200
150
130
Dungeon Ghyll Force
Mark Gate
FB
Fall
Millbeck
New Hotel
White Crag
Waterfall
Gravel Gill
3
Raven Crag
Weir
FB
Rossett
Kirk Howe
2
C
92
Sheepfold
Middle Fell Farm
Rossett Bridge
Side House
S
343
Ford
106
97
Stool End
Bield
Wall End
Oxendale Beck
Resr
Weir
Oxendale
FB
Redacre Gill
Cairns
Bield
Side Pike
224
Cattle Grid

2 **C** ***Middlefell Buttress* (76m, Diff, J Laycock, S.W. Herford, A.R. Thomson, 1911)**

There are several alternative starts. The traditional one up the chimney at the left end of the buttress (right of the gate) is no longer recommended due to unstable blocks. This warning also affects the sporting chimney on the left side of the buttress just through the gate. The wall can be tackled direct, either by the fingery crack right of the traditional chimney start or by the obvious left-slanting crack, but both are hard – up to VS standard. The recommended start is as follows:

P1 **16m:** Climb the wall at the right-hand end of the buttress, about 15m right of the old chimney start. A thin crack rises discontinuously up the wall; climbing begins on good holds just to the left of the crack. On cresting the wall scramble left, rejoining the traditional line, and continue up to a large terrace.

Middlefell Buttress, a variety of starts.

P2 **45m:** A slabby wall leads to a romp up the rounded arête to a grassy neck and block belay. Walk up grass and re-belay below a steep wall.

P3 **15m:** The wall yields most easily if tackled up the break from right to left. Continue up cracks and a short corner to a shelf where the buttress lays back into fellside. Coil the rope.

3 Walk directly up the grassy nose and fellside until a thin path is reached at *c*.460m. Turn left and follow the path up past a cairn to a brow at *c*.512m. Leave the main path and traverse the fellside northward to cross Dungeon Ghyll beck, joining a path which angles up the fellside, crosses a path descending from Thorn Crag, and then drops gently down to Stickle Tarn.

It is not necessary to follow this path all the way to Stickle Tarn. Some height loss can be saved by taking a high traverse line above the west side of the tarn. Aim for the foot of the arête of *Crescent Climb*, now in full view.

Climbing the wall on the recommended start.

Catherine Kenyon enjoying *Middlefell Buttress*.

4 **C** ***Crescent Climb* (100m, Mod, F Botterill, W.E. Palmer, 1907)**

Crescent Climb is etched in dirty white on the dark face of Pavey; an arête rising from the centre of the foot of the crag and a dipping traverse above a blank-looking slab.

P1 48m: From the foot of the vegetated Crescent Gully, climb the arête on its right hand side. Some of the rock is loose – take care not to bombard those below. Belay on a platform that has two old pegs hammered into a crack – sound enough in 2012 but best backed up.

P2 25m: Climb vegetated rock above to a good belay below a wall. Step down carefully to the right to traverse beneath a bulging wall. A sling can be threaded beneath a jammed rock – although there are positive holds across the traverse, the exposure is mouth-drying and the protection most reassuring, particularly for your second. Belay at a stance at the right end of the traverse.

P3 27m: Climb easily up vegetated rocks – running belays in the crack on the left and around a rowan trunk – to *Jack's Rake*; belay on a block at the back of the *Rake*.

Pavey Ark.

5 **C** ***Gwynne's Chimney*** **(24m, Diff, H.A. Gwynne and companions, 1892)**

The obvious chimney about 5m right of the top of *Crescent Climb* is a classic of the genre, dirty, slippery when wet, and infuriating with a rucksack, but for devotees of chimneys the only way to the top of Pavey Ark.

The chimney itself yields after about 20m and one can launch right and belay before continuing up the rib. Above, the climbing is more broken, but a satisfying line can be pieced together, mainly to the right of the gully.

6 Pavey Ark (700m). From the summit rocks, a path undulates west and south-west to a junction where our route ascends south to Harrison Stickle.

7 Harrison Stickle (736m). Descend west to a junction at *c.*640m and take a path trending south-east in impressive terrain, crags on the left and the defile of Dungeon Ghyll on the right. Continue down open fellside, eventually to a stile at *c.*165m. Cross this into a field and a couple of minutes later turn sharp right over a footbridge and follow the bridleway back to the Old Dungeon Ghyll.

Alternative finishes: Omitting *Gwynne's Chimney*, either scramble up *Jack's Rake* from the top of *Crescent Climb* or descend the *Rake* to Stickle Tarn. For those going up, the *Rake* continues from the top of *Crescent* via grooves, terraces and rough-textured slabs, eventually curving right to finish at a broken wall. From here the top of Pavey Ark is just a few metres right (east). Meanwhile, descending the *Rake* requires care; trench-like in places, it is a natural drainage line. From Stickle Tarn, follow the major path that descends from the south side to the New Dungeon Ghyll Hotel. If returning to the ODG, turn right just above the hotel and follow the bridleway referred to in **Point 7**.

Terry Gifford savouring *Bowfell Buttress.*

13 Bowfell Buttress & Crinkle Crags

13km V Diff/HS

Challenging climb at the head of Great Langdale

OLD DUNGEON GHYLL – MICKLEDEN – *Bowfell Buttress,* V Diff/HS **– BOW FELL – CRINKLE CRAGS – OXENDALE – OLD DUNGEON GHYLL**

The day

The classic route on Bowfell Buttress is defined by its notorious 'Slippery Crack'. As you struggle to maintain contact with its polished sides you may ask yourself how this route came to be included in a book of ostensibly 'easy' climbs? Or maybe you won't. The intensity of the moment as you slap and stretch for some elusive hand-hold is likely to drive out all incidental thought.

But fear not. Eventually one in the party will force a way up the crack to more reasonable climbing above and benightment will be avoided. And it's not necessarily a horror show – the buttress may be bone dry, you match fit, and you'll cruise it. Just be aware: the Slippery Crack has frustrated many a climber for whom *Bowfell Buttress* should have been way beneath his or her climbing grade.

Bowfell Buttress rises at the head of Great Langdale, the northernmost of a cirque of crags on the east rim of Bow Fell. More than a simple buttress, it is an imposing 100-metre-high crag blessed with string of good climbs, most of them much harder than the classic with which it shares its name.

Grading *Bowfell Buttress* has long been a doubtful business. Traditionally it has been given 'V Diff' but with heavy qualifications about the awkwardness of the Slippery Crack. Years of flailing limbs have given a sheen to what little purchase there is and only the presence of a commodious grass ledge at the foot of the crack preserved its modest grading – that is, until 2013 when the new FRCC *Langdale* guide up-rated it to Hard Severe.

Both on paper and in reality, *Bowfell Buttress* is thus the hardest route in this book. It is also one of the most satisfying. The climb weaves up the front of the triangular buttress, mixing grooves, short chimneys and slabs, almost to the top of the mountain. Savour the situation, (easier while belaying!) poised on one of the highest cliffs in the Lake District, looking out to the Langdale Pikes with Mickleden at your feet.

The summit is only a short walk away, a rough mound of tumbled boulders and, at 902 metres, the highest of the horseshoe of hills enclosing Langdale. Needless to say, the view is comprehensive. Descent is via Three Tarns col, from where a well-worn path down The Band offers the quickest route back to the ODG. Better by far though is to traverse the rocky undulations of Crinkle Crags. This will mean down-climbing the so-called 'Bad Step', however, having negotiated the Slippery Crack, this three-metre broken wall will be a piece of cake.

BOWFELL BUTTRESS & CRINKLE CRAGS

DISTANCE: 13km **TOTAL ASCENT:** *c.*1,040m **START:** Old Dungeon Ghyll GR: NY 286061 **TIME:** Allow at least 8hrs **CLIMBING:** *Bowfell Buttress* 110m, mainly V Diff, crux Hard Severe **SCRAMBLING:** Short bits possible over the Crinkles, notably 3m descent of Bad Step at Grade 1 **MAP:** OS Explorer OL6: The English Lakes South-western area, 1:25000 **REFRESHMENTS:** In Great Langdale: Old Dungeon Ghyll Hotel (T: 015394 37272); Sticklebarn Tavern (T: 015394 37356); and New Dungeon Ghyll Hotel (T: 015394 37213)

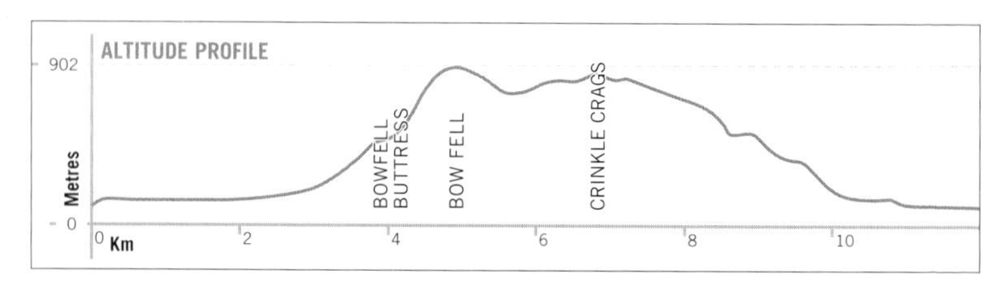

The Route

Bowfell Buttress & Crinkle Crags

Start

Old Dungeon Ghyll Hotel. Parking is available in the National Trust car park by the hotel at the head of Great Langdale (usually busy – more parking near the New Dungeon Ghyll). There is also a bus stop: service from Ambleside. **GR: NY 286061.**

S Old Dungeon Ghyll, Great Langdale. Pass behind the hotel and go through a gate on to a track heading west, then north-west, up Mickleden.

2 At a junction by a cairn, just after crossing a footbridge over Stake Gill beck, *c.*3km from the hotel, bear left to follow the Rossett Gill path.

3 After staying fairly close to the gill, the path angles away from it, up leftwards. At the point where the path turns back sharp right (*c.*500m) leave the path and continue angling up leftwards over grass and rocks, aiming for the foot of the buttress, prominent to the right of a scree gully.

ROUTE CONTINUES OVERLEAF

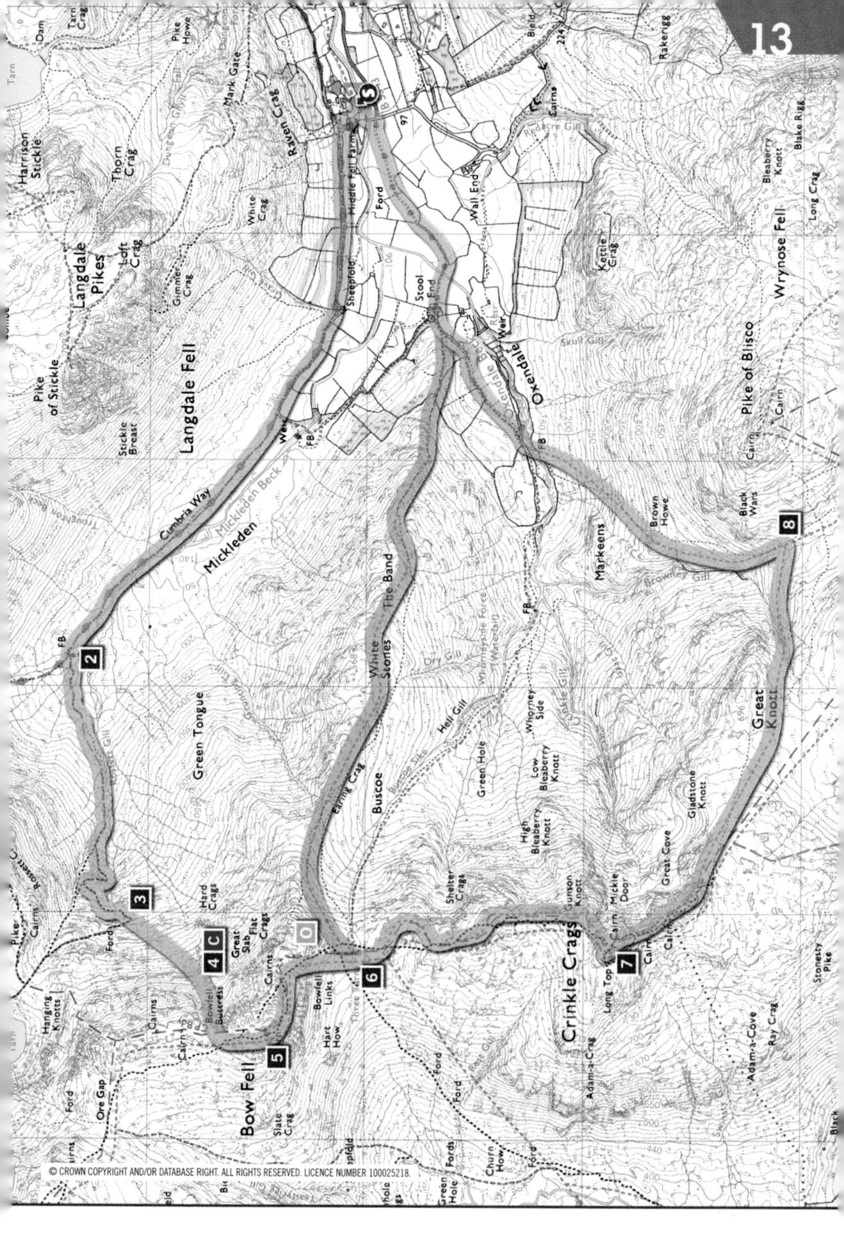
13
Langdale Pikes
Langdale Fell
Pike of Stickle
Harrison Stickle
Thorn Crag
Loft Crag
Gimmer Crag
Stickle Breast
Raven Crag
White Crag
Mark Gate
Pike Howe
Middle Fell Farm
Sheepfold
Stool End
Wall End
Oxendale
Skull Gill
Redacre Gill
Kettle Crag
Wrynose Fell
Pike of Blisco
Bleaberry Knott
Blake Rigg
Long Crag
Rakerigg
Brown Howe
Black Wars
Markeens
Browney Gill
Great Knott
Gladstone Knott
Great Cove
Mickle Door
Gunson Knott
Crinkle Crags
Long Top
Adam-a-Crag
Adam-a-Cove
Ray Crag
Stonesty Pike
Whorneyside Force (Waterfall)
Whorney Side
Hell Gill
Green Hole
Low Bleaberry Knott
High Bleaberry Knott
Shelter Crags
Buscoe
Buscoe Sike
Earing Crag
White Stones
The Band
Mickleden
Mickleden Beck
Cumbria Way
Green Tongue
Hard Crags
Great Slab
Flat Crags
Bowfell Buttress
Bowfell Links
Hart How
Bow Fell
Slate Crag
Ore Gap
Hanging Knotts
Three Tarns
Churn How
Cairns
Ford
FB
Weir
S
2
3
4
C
5
6
7
8
© CROWN COPYRIGHT AND/OR DATABASE RIGHT. ALL RIGHTS RESERVED. LICENCE NUMBER 100025218.

4 **C** *Bowfell Buttress* **(110m, mainly V Diff, crux Hard Severe, T Shaw, G.H. Craig, G.R. West, C Hargreaves, L.J. Oppenheimer, 1902)**

Start at a scoop just left of the steep wall that forms the base of the crag.

P1 23m: Climb the scoop and its right-hand edge to the base of a short polished chimney/crack on the right. (Good belay here; pitch could be split.) Though little more than 3m, this awkward feature is every bit as slippery as the Slippery Crack and demands a 'go for it' approach – particularly by shorties. Holds are high on the right.

Move easily right to belay on the terrace.

P2 35m: A pleasant pitch with no nasty surprises. Climb the wall above the ledge, initially steeply and delicately, trending left to the 'sentry box' below a stepped chimney. (Possible belay here.) Ascend the chimney or the rib on the right for 12m, then easy ledges to another terrace. Walk down the slope rightwards to the foot of a steep wall with the infamous crack.

P3 17m: Tackle the Slippery Crack (*c*.6m) with vigour, left foot in the crack, handhold high in the crack; from about half height there are small edges for feet to the right of the crack. Pull over the top and move up right over slabs to a pinnacle belay.

Bowfell Buttress.

P4 **18m:** Trend left to a groove that turns to a chimney; up a slab and short wall then step up leftwards across the corner to belay on a large ledge.

P5 **17m:** Ascend the deep groove on the right; where this forks, take the left branch to finish.

From the top of the buttress (Low Man) cross the col to the main massif and head southwards up the bouldery slope to the summit of Bow Fell.

5 Bow Fell (902m). After admiring the view, descend generally south-east to Three Tarns.

6 Three Tarns (*c.*730m). From a broad col walk southwards on braided path(s), on to Shelter Crags and then undulating over the Crinkles.

O Alternatively, for a shorter, direct return to the ODG, go eastwards from Three Tarns and down The Band to Stool End Farm.

7 From the Fourth or Great Crinkle (Long Top, 859m), descend southwards by the scrambly 'Bad Step' – a broken 3m wall – into a gully. Trending south-east, continue down for 2km to a path junction north of Red Tarn.

8 At the junction turn left and follow the path northwards down to cross Oxendale Beck and continue on to Stool End. A farm road over meadows leads to the Old Dungeon Ghyll Hotel, car park and bus stop.

Nigel Jenkins on pitch 1 of *Bowfell Buttress.*

Paul Goulding tackles the 'Slippery Crack'.

Steve Lenartowicz seeks out the cleanest line on Great Carrs Buttress.

14 Greenburn Circuit

12km Grade 1/2

Scrambling in the wake of Vikings, miners and unlucky bombers

FELL FOOT, LITTLE LANGDALE – GREENBURN MINE – *Long Crag,* Grade 1/2 **– WETHERLAM – SWIRL HAWSE – GREAT CARRS – WET SIDE EDGE – FELL FOOT**

The day

The little-visited Greenburn valley above Little Langdale offers free-roaming scrambling on cleanish rock in a landscape rich in Lakeland history. Yet neither the rock nor the history is glaringly obvious. Greenburn is a quiet, subtle place; somewhere for those of an inquiring mind to piece together the past while exploring the rough crags below Wetherlam and Great Carrs.

This a 'light sack' day; no rope or other climbing gear is required and the broken nature of the crags and craglets allows the scrambling to be adjusted to taste: difficulties can simply be bypassed. The first of the scrambles, *Long Crag,* is a satisfying valley-to-summit ascent and the second, on Great Carrs, can be left out if time, energy or the weather suggests it.

Fell Foot lies at the eastern foot of the Wrynose Pass and sees far more motorists and cyclists, straining over the Wrynose and Hardknott passes, than it does pedestrians.

Only a handful of those braking on the bends by Fell Foot Farm will realise that just over a wall behind the farm is the site of a Viking meeting place. The 'Ting Mound', now in the care of the National Trust, is said to have been either a parliament or court.

Entering Greenburn above the south bank of its lovely beck, it is hard to imagine that the valley was an industrial site in Victorian times. But here is the ruined engine house and waterwheel pit, and high on the north flank of Wetherlam are levels where copper was mined until 1917. Long Crag rises up the same hillside in a series of broken low crags and easy-angled slabs to barely 100 metres below Wetherlam's top.

Turning west from Wetherlam, our route now describes a horseshoe high above Greenburn, with Great Carrs at its head. The eager scrambler will probably traverse from Swirl Hawse to the foot of the left buttress of Great Carrs. But there is certainly no anti-climax in continuing over Swirl How, at 802 metres the highest point on the circuit and with one of the finest panoramas in the Lake District. Just beyond, above Broad Slack, is a poignant reminder from a more recent past – a memorial of stones and aircraft wreckage commemorating eight Canadian airmen who perished when their Halifax LL505 clipped the col on 22 October 1944. More wreckage is strewn below in Broad Slack.

GREENBURN CIRCUIT

DISTANCE: 12km **TOTAL ASCENT:** *c.*1,000m (if the Great Carrs scramble is included)
START: Fell Foot Bridge GR: NY 300032 **TIME:** 6.5–8hrs **CLIMBING:** None **SCRAMBLING:** *Long Crag* 300m, Grade 1/2; *Great Carrs Buttress* 220m, Grade 2 **MAP:** OS Explorer OL4: The English Lakes North-western area, 1:25000
REFRESHMENTS: Three Shires Inn, Little Langdale (T: 015394 37215)

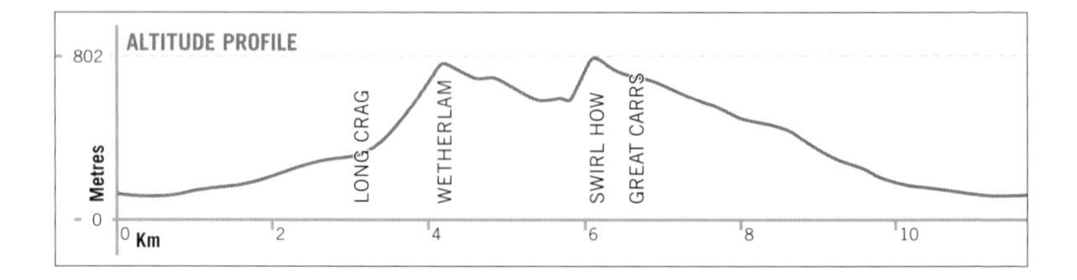

The Route **Greenburn Circuit**

Start

Fell Foot Bridge, 2km west of Little Langdale village. Limited parking in pull-offs on the Wrynose Pass road beyond Fell Foot Farm. **GR: NY 300032.**

S From Fell Foot Bridge, a track signed *Public Way Tilberthwaite* leaves the road just east of Fell Foot Farm and immediately crosses the infant River Brathay. Follow the Tilberthwaite track past Bridge End (cottage), through a gate and onwards for another 200m before doubling back on a good mine track heading west-south-west up the Greenburn valley. The mine ruins are reached 2km from this junction.

2 From the mine buildings, Long Crag is clearly visible to the south-west, forming a discontinuous craggy skyline descending from Wetherlam. The lowest point of the crag is about 100m above the altitude of the mine and directly south of the silted-up Greenburn reservoir. If dry underfoot, a rising traverse can be made across the fell from the mine; otherwise follow the south bank of the beck to the reservoir and walk directly up the hillside to the crag.

ROUTE CONTINUES OVERLEAF

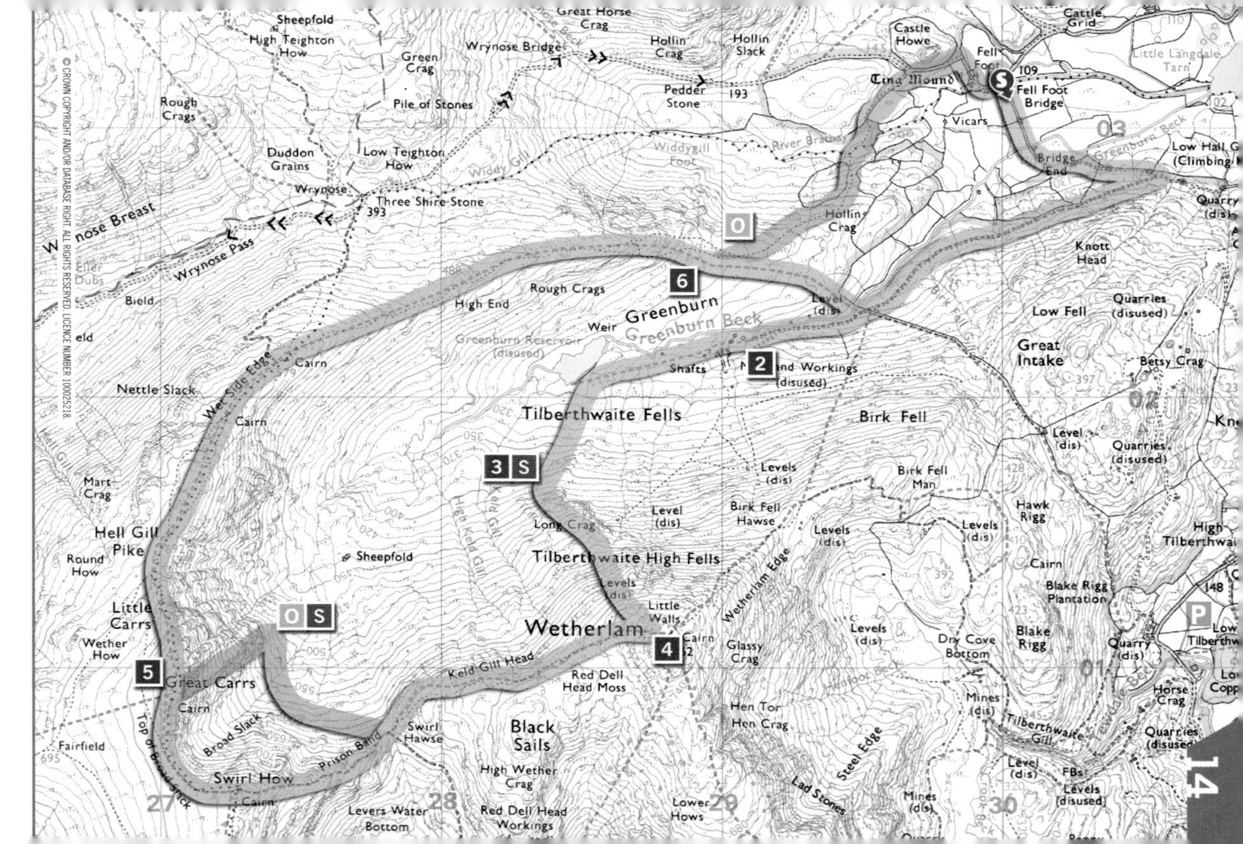

Wetherlam
Tilberthwaite High Fells
Tilberthwaite Fells
Birk Fell
Greenburn
Greenburn Beck
Greenburn Reservoir (disused)
Great Carrs
Swirl How
Black Sails
Hell Gill Pike
Little Carrs
Wet Side Edge
Wetherlam Edge
Steel Edge
Lad Stones
Fell Foot Bridge
Castle Howe
Ting Mound
Hollin Crag
Pedder Stone
Three Shire Stone
Wrynose Pass
Wrynose Bridge
Pile of Stones
Rough Crags
High End
Great Intake
Low Fell
Knott Head
Blake Rigg
Hawk Rigg
Birk Fell Man
Birk Fell Hawse
Red Dell Head Moss
Keld Gill Head
Swirl Hawse
Prison Band
Top of Broad Slack
Great Horse Crag
Hollin Slack
Long Crag
Sheepfold

3 **S** *Long Crag* **(300m, Grade 1/2)**

A small pile of stones – 'cairn' would be too grand a term – beneath a blunt nose marks the traditional start. This is not particularly obvious. Some 15m to the right is a rowan tree; 20m lower, to the left, is a smaller rowan. However this is terrain that allows the scrambler plenty of scope to choose his or her own line. An equally attractive start can be made *c.*20m left of the cairn on clean slabs and bulges. (To underline this free-roaming approach, I don't think my companion and I stepped on the same rock as each other at any point on the whole climb.)

Rather than a single crag, the route links a succession of craglets. The second is distinguished by a 10m wall at its left end and has a solitary juniper on a ledge above. Though tempting, the wall is best resisted unless you have confidence solo climbing at about Severe. Easier rock lies to the right. From the top of this outcrop descend slightly across a grass gully to gain a rib and link slabs and bulges until clean rock peters out.

You are now at about 540m and must traverse leftwards to resume the climb, crossing two bands of scree and scrabbling up to where a small section of wall hides an old mine working. The nose above can be gained from either the left or right side of this recess; slabs and short steps lead to the top of the scramble at *c.*650m from where a 15-minute walk up lands you on Wetherlam (762m).

You have been warned!

Julian Cooper stitching the outcrops of Long Crag.

Long Crag upper section.

Long Crag lower section.

Steve Lenartowicz on Great Carrs Buttress.

The Halifax LL505 memorial.

Great Carrs.

4 From the summit cairn a well-worn path leads west-south-west to Swirl Hawse (*c*.615m). **You now have a choice**. If scrambling, descend north-west from here, across Broad Slackfor the scramble up *Great Carrs Buttress*. **Otherwise**, continue up Prison Band to Swirl How (802m) and then swing northwards, past the memorial to the Halifax bomber crew, to the cairn on the lip of Great Carrs.

O **S** ***Great Carrs Buttress* (220m, Grade 2)**

Turn right at the cairn on Swirl Hawse and pause for a few minutes to get your bearings. *Great Carrs Buttress* dominates the view to the north-west, descending steeply at first from the summit and easing into a ridge of small outcrops and grass. The scramble begins at around 550m at a clean outcrop with a flying saucer-shaped block perched on its top edge.

A faint path angles leftwards into Broad Slack (the cwm that forms the head of Greenburn valley) then peters out. The perched block is hard to spot from above but comes into plain view as the foot of the scramble nears.

Climb the blunt end of the first outcrop either from a grass rake on its left or more directly if you've come prepared for rock climbing. Here, as elsewhere on this scramble, there is no definitive route, simply pick a line on the cleanest rock – there is moss in places – according to how bold you are feeling.

Short ribs lead to a grass slope at approximately half height. Traverse right across scree and scramble up rock steps, trending rightwards. Cross the top of a gully to a fissured rib, climbed on good flakes. A steep, spiky arête leads to the top. Unfortunately these higher rocks are usually greasy. There is easier ground on a rib just a few metres to the right across a stony gully.

5 Great Carrs (780m). After visiting the Halifax bomber cairn, head north from the summit and soon swing eastwards, keeping to the crest of Wet Side Edge, the fine grassy ridge that encloses the north side of the Greenburn valley.

6 The main path of the grassy ridge eventually descends to the footbridge over Greenburn Beck – 3.5km from Great Carrs. There is a choice of finishes. Continue on the path to cross the beck and rejoin the outward mine track back to Fell Foot Bridge.

O Alternatively, at just below 300m on the ridge (GR: NY 290025) bear off left and pick up an indistinct path (a few weathered cairns confirm the way but not at first); descend by the stone wall of a small enclosure, ford the infant River Brathay and pick up a track that soon leads to the Wrynose Pass road, 200m west of the Ting Mound at Fell Foot.

3

Dow, Wasdale & the South-West Lakes

On a fine day few crags in England can beat Dow Crag, Coniston: the two classic climbs featured here are suffused in big cliff atmosphere. Beyond lies the wild west, including a climb to the highest point in England, Scafell Pike, via the continuously absorbing V Diff, *Grooved Arête*, and a challenging route on Steeple Buttress, above Ennerdale, that qualifies as exploration.

Julian Davey pads up *Giant's Crawl*, Dow Crag. Goat's Water lies below.

The rock climber's 'happy hunting ground' – Dow Crag.

15 **Dow Crag Circuit** 8km Diff

Classic climbs on south Lakeland's biggest cliff

WALNA SCAR ROAD – GOAT'S WATER – DOW CRAG (*C Ordinary, Easy Terrace, Giant's Crawl,* all Diff) – **BUCK PIKE – BLIND TARN – WALNA SCAR ROAD**

The day

Dow Crag has been a favourite of Lake District climbers for more than a century. Though its proud elevation, open to whatever blows in from the Irish Sea and Morecambe Bay, can render the crag out of bounds for days on end, when the sun shines there are few better places for rock climbing than Dow.

The two routes chosen for this tour of the crag – *C Ordinary* and *Giant's Crawl* – have entertained climbers for generations; in dry conditions both are comfortable Diffs, with *Giant's Crawl* just having the edge in seriousness and satisfaction. They are linked here by a descent of *Easy Terrace*, popular as a scrambling route up the mountain.

Dow Crag was known as 'Doe Crag' (a reference, perhaps, to a haunt of deer?) when Owen Glynne Jones wrote his classic *Rock Climbing in the English Lake District* in 1897, describing the crag as 'this happy hunting-ground for the rock-climber'. It is the biggest crag in southern Lakeland, its five buttresses soaring above scree slopes, facing east across Goat's Water cove to the Old Man of Coniston.

Unusually, Dow combines the qualities of a high crag with easy accessibility. It is only one hour's walk from the end of the tarmac on the Walna Scar Road, above Coniston, to the foot of the climbs. Thus it seldom feels remote; the crag echoes to the shouts of other climbers, while below, walkers file past Goat's Water en route to or from the Old Man.

Had Jones written his guide seven years later, he could have included *C Ordinary*, one of five new routes pioneered by G.F. and A.J. Woodhouse in August 1904 – a time when climbers were moving out from Dow's gullies to begin exploring the buttresses. Five years later, the Addyman brothers and Stobart put up *Giant's Crawl*, which has the bonus of finishing a short walk from the mountain summit.

To be savoured to the full, these two fine trad climbs deserve reserving for a spell of dry, and preferably sunny, weather. From your stances on the crag, the eyes will be drawn southwards across the Furness peninsula to the sea. But that's where the southwesterlies blow in from. Also while Dow rock, a volcanic type called rhyolite, is generally sound and a pleasure to climb on, it quickly becomes slippery when wet. *C Ordinary* then becomes far from ordinary, and the *Giant's Crawl* risks becoming a slide.

DOW CRAG CIRCUIT

DISTANCE: 8km **TOTAL ASCENT:** *c.*700m **START:** Foot of Walna Scar Track GR: SD 289970 **TIME:** 8.5hrs
CLIMBING: *C Ordinary, Giant's Crawl*, total 195m, Diff **SCRAMBLING:** *Easy Terrace*, in descent, -75m, Grade: 2/3
MAP: OS Explorer OL6: The English Lakes South-western area, 1:25000
REFRESHMENTS: The Sun Inn (T: 015394 41248); and other pubs and cafes in Coniston

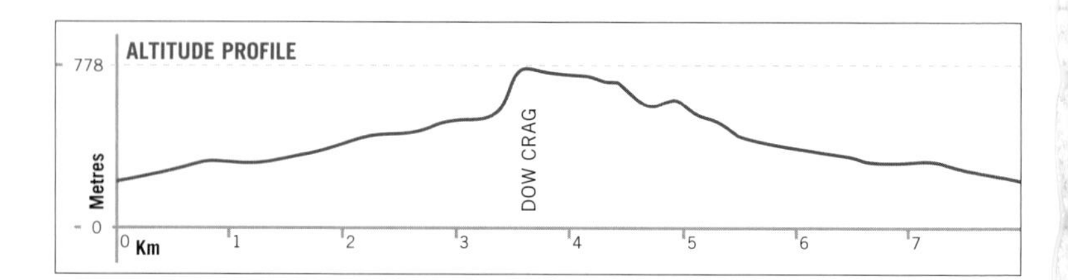

The Route **Dow Crag Circuit**

Start

Start at the foot of Walna Scar Road above Coniston, reached via a steep, narrow road running south-west from the village for 1.5km. Though called Walna Scar 'Road' on the OS map, it is actually a rough track. Parking is to either side of this track, just the through the gate where the metalled road ends. **GR: SD 289970.**

S Follow the track west-south-west for almost 2km.

2 Branch right (north-west) on the footpath heading to Goat's Water and the Old Man.

3 Bear left off the main path, ford the outflow stream from Goat's Water and pick up an indistinct 'path' that weaves through boulders near the tarn before angling up scree to the foot of Dow Crag.

The crag's five main buttresses are tagged A, B, C, D, E, from left to right. Aim for C buttress, which rises right of the blue 'rescue box' beneath B buttress (see topo, overleaf).

ROUTE CONTINUES OVERLEAF

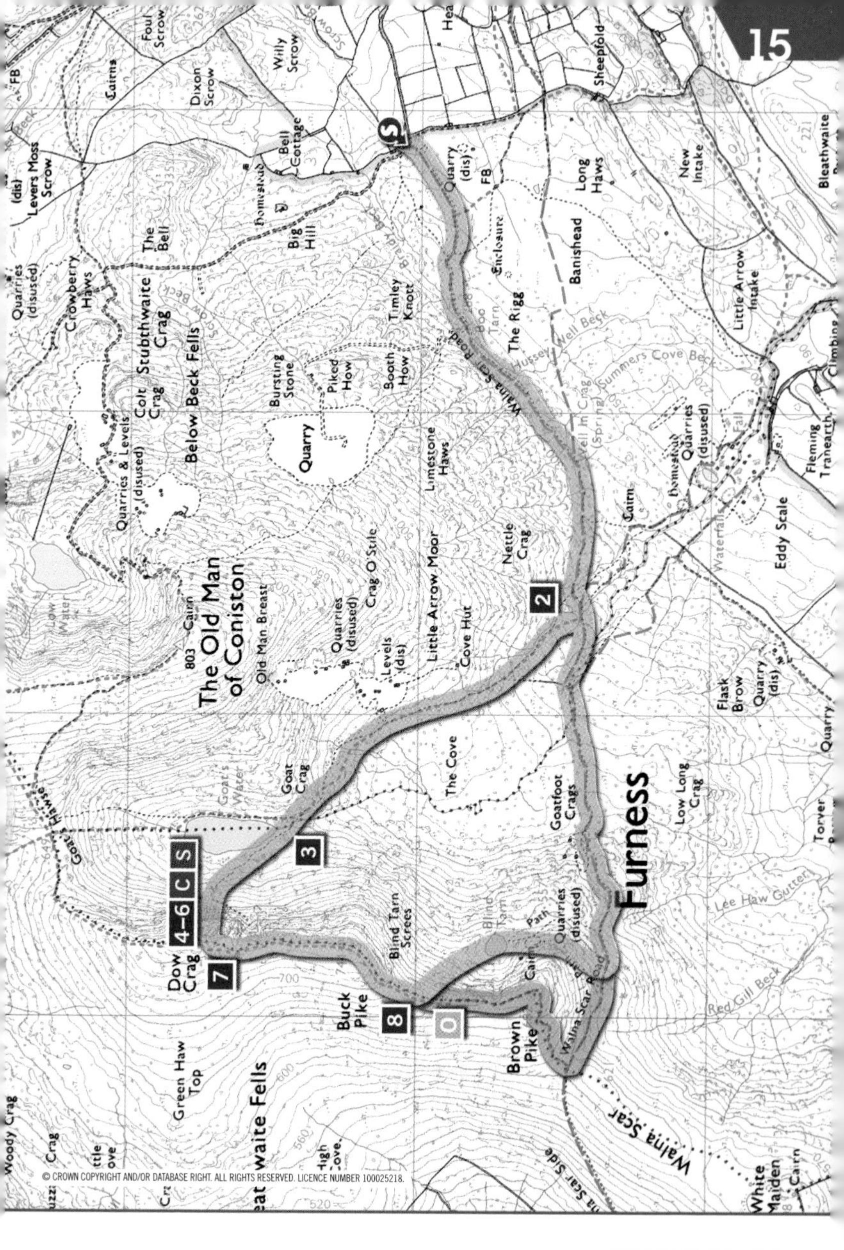
15
The Old Man of Coniston
803
Cairn
Old Man Breast
Furness
Dow Crag
Buck Pike
Brown Pike
Goat's Water
Goat Crag
Blind Tarn Screes
Blind Tarn
Walna Scar Road
Walna Scar
The Cove
Cove Hut
Little Arrow Moor
Crag O'Stile
Nettle Crag
Limestone Haws
Quarry
Bursting Stone
Piked How
Booth How
Timley Knott
Big Hill
The Bell
Below Beck Fells
Stubthwaite Crag
Colt Crag
Crowberry Haws
Quarries & Levels (disused)
Low Water
Goat's Hawse
Green Haw Top
Goatfoot Crags
Quarries (disused)
Levels (dis)
Bell Cottage
Homestead
Willy Scrow
Dixon Scrow
Foul Scrow
Levers Moss Scrow
Sheepfold
The Rigg
Enclosure
Banishead
Long Haws
New Intake
Little Arrow Intake
Hussey Well Beck
Summers Cove Beck
Fleming Tranearth
Eddy Scale
Flask Brow
Low Long Crag
Torver
Lee Haw Gutter
Red Gill Beck
White Maiden
Woody Crag
2
3
4–6
C
S
7
8
0

4 **C** *C Ordinary* **(80m, Diff, G.F. & A.J. Woodhouse, 1904)**

Start just left of the foot of C buttress – the lowest point of the whole crag.

P1 16m: Follow the inviting crack-line up the broad base of the buttress, move left to pass three small overhangs, and continue up the crest of the buttress and on to a long flake.

Several variations of the line and belays are possible, for example, Pitches 1 and 2 can be combined.

P2 10m: A scoop leads to easier ground and on to a commodious ledge below a steep wall with another scoop on the left.

P3 20m: Follow the scoop rightwards to a ledge, then leftwards over slabs to the edge of the buttress. Continue up ledges to a stance just beneath the lip of an extensive slab.

P4 10m: Climb onto the slab and pad up rightwards in a fine position to ledges.

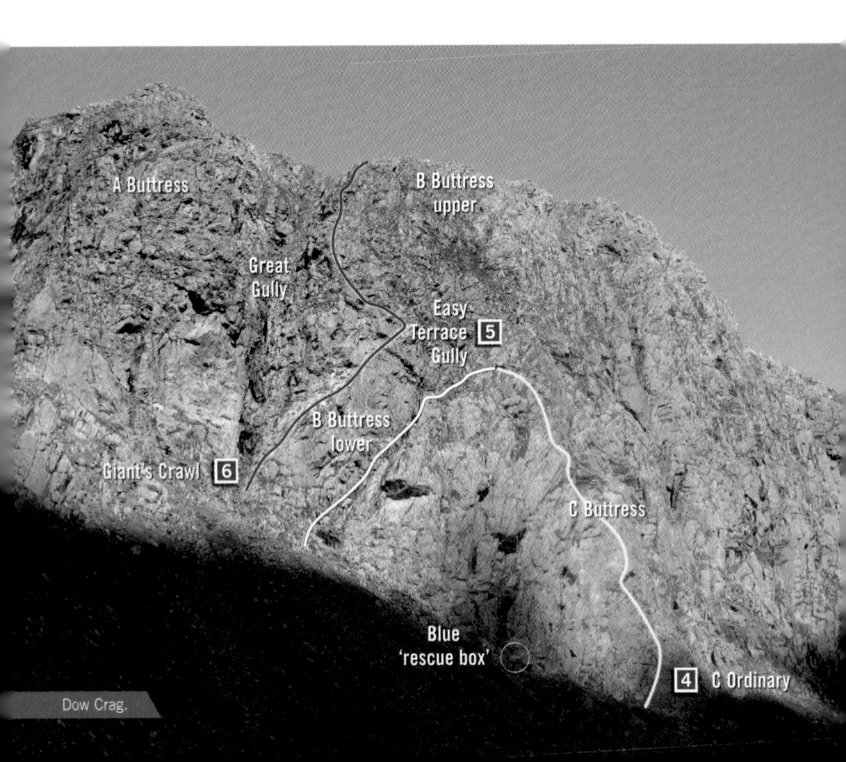

Dow Crag.

P5 14m: Work left on flakes, duck under the prow, tackle a short, polished crack, and step up a few moves higher to a ledge and belay.

P5 10m: Move rightwards over slabs to a ledge; continue along the gangway to a second ledge, then go up to the traverse line. Follow this leftwards to easier ground and a scramble to the top.

5 S *Easy Terrace* (in descent, -75m, Grade 2/3)

Follow the grass terrace leftwards. This runs horizontally then tips downwards into a gully bisecting B Buttress into its upper and lower sections. Stay on the left lip (in descent) of the gully at first before scrambling down into its bed.

Emerging from this gully, turn right and go up over rubbly ledges beneath B Buttress towards Great Gully to the foot of *Giant's Crawl*.

Phil Blanshard sets out on *C Ordinary*.

Descending from *Easy Terrace*.

6 **C** ***Giant's Crawl* (115m, Diff, E.T.W. & O.T. Addyman, Stobart, 1909)**

A superior route to *C Ordinary*. Less variation in the line though pitches may be apportioned differently. Start up the broad slabby gangway that angles up rightwards from the right-hand side of the mouth of Great Gully.

P1 35m: Climb slabs and move left to the foot of the crack. (Belay here to split the pitch.) Climb the crack through a quartz zone to a slanting ledge and follow this to a belay at its right-hand end.

P2 30m: This is the pitch that makes *Giant's Crawl* special. A short wall leads to the 'Narrows' – stepped slabs creating a gangway that narrows as it climbs into the void midway up the cliff. This is also a place of potential congestion, not just with parties on the *Crawl* but climbers on other B Buttress routes that cross here. Continue to easy ground as the Narrows level out and the steep wall above lays back into a tumbled bay.

P3 18m: Go up to an earthy terrace and move up leftwards to a corner crack – awkward to start but soon dispatched by a vigorous approach. Do not get too embedded in the crack. Pull on to a large ledge overlooking Great Gully.

A delectable swimming hole: Blind Tarn below Brown Pike.

P4 **12m:** Move left and slightly down to a ledge at the foot of a groove. Climb this on jammed flakes and exit right.

P5 **20m:** Easy climbing and scrambling to the top of the buttress.

Walk up the slope to the main massif, turn right on the ridge-top path and walk and scramble to the rocky summit.

7 Dow Crag (778m). Descend south and follow the ridge path over Buck Pike (744m).

8 To pass by the mountain jewel of Blind Tarn, descend the east side of the ridge on a steep grassy slope and angle across the hillside to the tarn. (Excellent for a dip after a hot day on the crag!) From the tarn, head south, picking up an old mine path that soon meets the Walna Scar Road. Turn left and follow the track for 3km eastwards to the starting point.

O Alternatively, from Point 8 continue south on to Brown Pike (682m) and descend south-west to Walna Scar Road on the felltop. Turn left and follow the track for 3.5km to the starting point.

Summit of Dow Crag. Julian Davey spots the way down.

The wilds of Upper Eskdale from the top of Ill Crag.

16 Upper Eskdale & Ill Crag 19km Grade 3

Top grade scrambling through an idyllic gorge and up a wild mountain face

BROTHERILKELD, ESKDALE – **LINGCOVE BRIDGE** – *Esk Gorge*, Grade 2 – **ILL CRAG** (*South-east Face*, Grade 3) – **ESK HAUSE** – **UPPER ESKDALE** – **BROTHERILKELD**

The day

Upper Eskdale comes nearer than perhaps anywhere else in the Lake District to being true wilderness. In all its wind-scoured vastness, the hand of man is barely visible – a tumbled sheep-fold, an ancient packhorse bridge, just the native rock rearranged centuries ago.

To either side of the infant Esk rise some of England's highest peaks, one of which, Ill Crag, offers one of the longest scrambles in the Lake District, and the most remote. Ill Crag is one of the three summits of the Scafell Pikes, the others being Broad Crag and Scafell 'Pike' itself, which, over time, has appropriated what once was a group name solely for its own use.

Of all the different valley aspects of these pikes, that from Eskdale is the finest: rocky coves and buttresses tumbling more than a thousand feet from the bare summits to the Great Moss and moraine mounds of the upper valley. But no '3-Peak baggers' come this way. A time-consuming approach on winding lanes from the far side of the Lakes and a long walk-in reserves Upper Eskdale for the determined connoisseur.

Commitment made, the scramble up the south-east face of Ill Crag will test your route-finding ability, plus your rock climbing skill if you opt for the most entertaining pitches; and before that comes the Esk gorge and the challenge of negotiating the margins of its deep pools and waterfalls without getting your feet wet, or worse.

If the sun is shining through the birches and rowans that overhang the gorge, spangling cascades and dappling eddies, it is an enchanted place. Indeed if the sun is *not* likely to be shining, and certainly if the weather is less than clement, Upper Eskdale is best avoided. The gorge scramble requires low water, and the ascent of Ill Crag reasonable visibility.

Unless you are bold solo rock climber, a rope and basic rack (nuts and slings) are advisable to make the best of the *South-east Face* route, though difficult passages can be bypassed. The two scrambles are likely to take a couple of hours each; factor in about ten miles of fairly rough walking, plus meal breaks and so on, and this is going to be a long day. But make an early start and keep to the cleanest rock by the water's edge and on Ill Crag and few outings could be more rewarding.

UPPER ESKDALE & ILL CRAG

DISTANCE: 19km **TOTAL ASCENT:** *c.*950m **START:** Brotherilkeld GR: NY 212012 **TIME:** 8–9hrs **CLIMBING:** None **SCRAMBLING:** *Esk Gorge c.*120m, Grade 2; *Ill Crag SE Face* c.320m, Grade 3 **MAP:** OS Explorer OL6: The English Lakes South-western area, 1:25000 **REFRESHMENTS:** Woolpack Inn, Eskdale (T: 019467 23230); also pubs at Boot and Eskdale Green

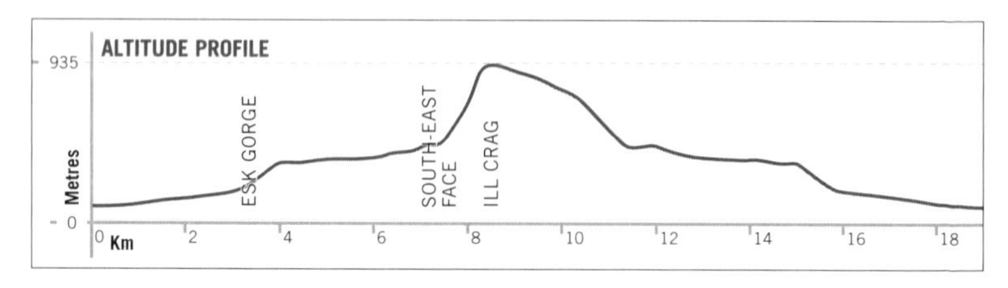

The Route

Upper Eskdale & Ill Crag

Start

Brotherilkeld, Eskdale, at the western foot of Hardknott Pass. Roadside parking west of a gateway by a phone box and road signs. There is also a small car park higher up, 100m east of the gateway. **GR: NY 212012.**

S At the western foot of Hardknott Pass are a cattle grid and a red telephone box by a gateway. A public footpath sign points down a track leading to Brotherilkeld Farm. Follow the track and just before the farm bear left on a path bypassing the buildings and continuing north-north-east on the east side of the Esk.

2 Lingcove Bridge, a picturesque packhorse bridge, is reached approximately 3km from the start. Cross the bridge over Lingcove Beck and prepare to enter the bed of the Esk on your left, just upstream of an impassable pool.

ROUTE CONTINUES OVERLEAF

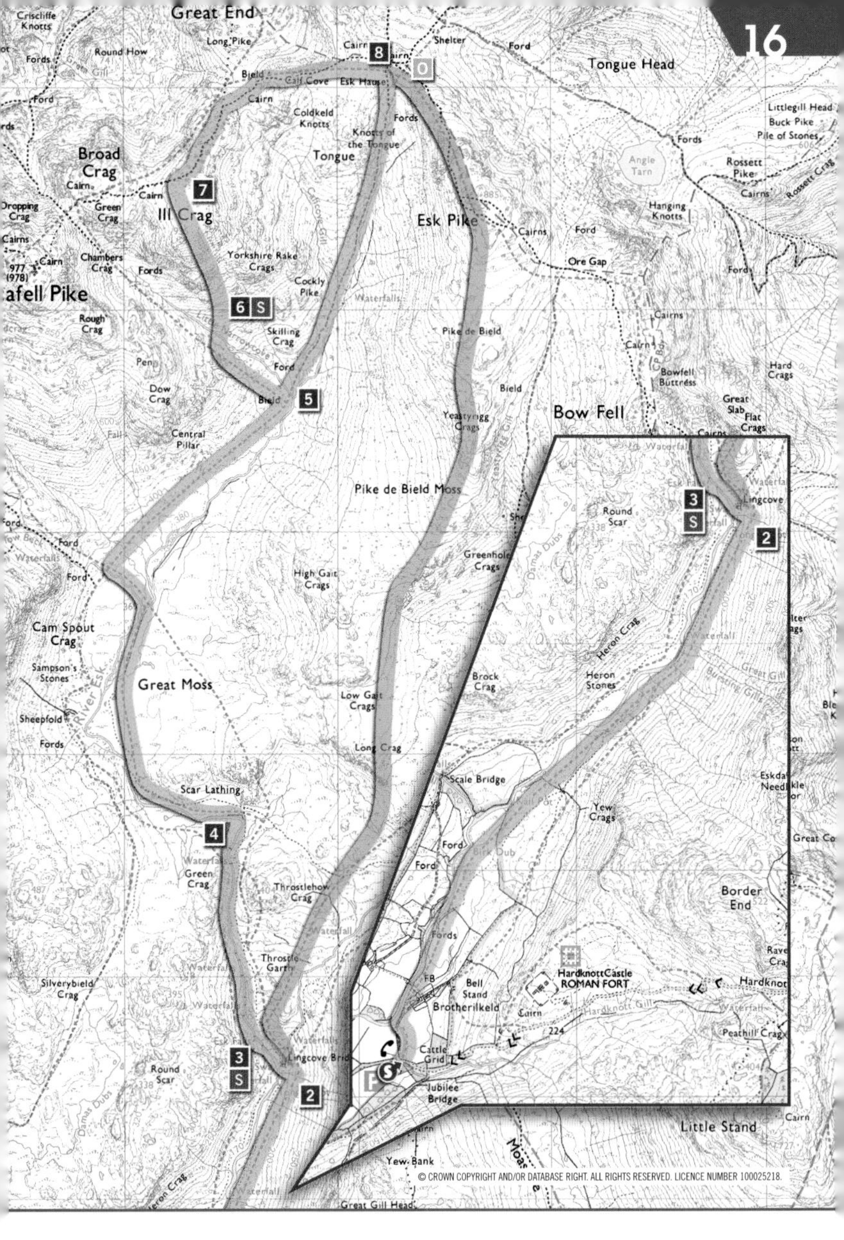

Great End
Long Pike
Round How
Fords
Bield
Calf Cove
Esk Hause
Shelter
Ford
Tongue Head
Cairn
Coldkeld Knotts
Knotts of the Tongue
Tongue
Fords
Broad Crag
Ill Crag
Esk Pike
Angle Tarn
Rossett Pike
Hanging Knotts
Ore Gap
Yorkshire Rake Crags
Cockly Pike
Skilling Crag
Pike de Bield
Bow Fell
Bowfell Buttress
Great Slab
Flat Crags
Pike de Bield Moss
Round Scar
Lingcove
Greenhole Crags
High Gait Crags
Heron Crag
Heron Stones
Brock Crag
Great Moss
Low Gait Crags
Long Crag
Cam Spout Crag
Sampson's Stones
River Esk
Sheepfold
Scar Lathing
Scale Bridge
Green Crag
Throstlehow Crag
Throstle Garth
Yew Crags
Border End
Silverybield Crag
Lingcove Bridge
Bell Stand
Brotherilkeld
Hardknott Castle ROMAN FORT
Cattle Grid
Jubilee Bridge
Little Stand
Yew Bank
Great Gill Head
Peathill Crag
Dow Crag
Central Pillar
Rough Crag
Chambers Crag
Crisclifffe Knotts
Tongue
© CROWN COPYRIGHT AND/OR DATABASE RIGHT. ALL RIGHTS RESERVED. LICENCE NUMBER 100025218.

3 S *Esk Gorge* (*c.*120m, generally Grade 2)

The gorge continues for about 1km, fairly open at first, then becoming deeper and more confined, with pools, cascades and waterfalls beckoning the scrambler upwards.

The general gill scrambling principle applies: keep as close to the waterline as possible; this is usually where the cleanest rock is to be found. However, although a pure line involves some wading, if you're intent on the full day out over Ill Crag, or are carrying a rope and climbing gear, try to avoid a soaking.

Rock-hopping from bank to bank, interest is maintained throughout, with two main passages of difficulty in the upper part: first a long deep pool traversed on the right wall, inches above the water, and second, the final waterfall. This last ascent is usually more honoured in the breach; its awkward shelves left for another day.

Descending into Upper Eskdale from Esk Hause.

4 Above the final waterfall, paths continue up the valley on either side of the Esk – that on the east bank, skirting the foot of Scar Lathing crag and then crossing the Great Moss, is marginally quicker. The moss is an easy place to get wet feet, although if the water in the gorge was low enough for scrambling, you may stay dry-shod over the moss. Once over the moss, cross the Esk and join the path heading north-east up the valley.

5 Turn north-west into Little Narrowcove, which rises between Scafell Pike and Ill Crag. The path is on the left side of the beck. Leave the path where the cove narrows and traverse across the beck to Ill Crag and to the foot of the slabs at approximately the 550m contour.

Scrambling up Esk Gorge: the art is in keeping your feet dry.

6 **S** ***Ill Crag South-east Face* (*c*.320m, Grade 2/3)**

A 320m mix of slabs, broken buttresses and grassy intervals weaving up the open face of the mountain. There is no prescriptive route, but there are three main features that comprise the best of the rock. A rope and a basic rack are recommended for the trickier lines on the central slabs and upper buttress, though easier alternatives can be found.

Start on stepped slabs that appear directly ahead, invitingly, as you traverse the cove. The slabs slant up leftwards at an easy angle. At the top of these ascend (walking) rightwards over grass and boulders, passing below a dark-streaked wall to a blocky rib approximately 30m below and right of a garden shed-sized boulder. Climb the rib on pleasingly rough rock, good friction and incut holds. At a steepening, step left of the arête and pull up a short awkward crack to easier-angled rock. Continue easily over bouldery steps and grass.

A clean 15m slab leads to a grassy terrace beneath the steeper 'central slabs'. Time, perhaps, to get the rope out. The best line starts up the centre of the slab, trends left and runs up the right edge of a heathery groove. Step left across the top of the groove to the edge of the buttress, then back right to follow the crest. A 50m rope will run from the bottom to top of the slabs, but only just.

Ill Crag.

From the top of the slabs scramble up leftwards over broken rocks and grass towards a deep mossy gully in the centre of the upper cliff. Below and right of the gully is a pedestal with a corner on its right. Ascend the groove in the right side of the corner to gain a nose above its steepest lower part. Continue up the rib. A grassy shoulder and scree leads to an easy-angled rib, followed almost to summit.

7 Ill Crag (935m). Various return routes are possible. Time may be getting short. The most straightforward – and used in the circuit details here – is to follow the stony felltop path north-east to Esk Hause. Taking the same path in the opposite direction, south-west, would lead first to the head of Little Narrowcove – offering a direct descent to the Esk – and then over Scafell Pike (978m) and a descent from Mickledore.

8 Esk Hause (759m). From the broad col a path drops south into a ravine and on down the west side of the infant Esk to join the outward route at the foot of Little Narrowcove. From Esk Hause to Brotherilkeld is approximately 9km.

O A more interesting alternative would be to ascend south-east from the Hause to Esk Pike (885m) and follow its long south ridge, eventually to Lingcove Bridge. This would entail another 100m of ascent.

Phil Blanshard on stepped slabs at the start of *Ill Crag South-east Face.*

Late sun burnishes the head of Wasdale; descending from a Scafell round.

17 Broad Stand & Scafell

12km Diff

Trembling line in a poet's corner

WASDALE HEAD – LINGMELL GILL – HOLLOW STONES – PIKES CRAG (*Crenation Ridge*, Diff) – **MICKLEDORE** – *Broad Stand*, Grade 3+ – **SCAFELL – GREEN HOW – BRACKENCLOSE – WASDALE HEAD**

The day

Few days are so finely etched in a climber's memory as those spent on Scafell Crag. From the beginnings of the sport in the nineteenth century to the present day, its gullies and – more notably – its soaring buttresses have held the grail for Lake District climbers.

However Scafell's two main faces – the beetling cliffs above Wasdale and the formidable East Buttress beyond Mickledore – are serious ground. Although there are one or two ostensibly 'easy' routes, such as *Slingsby's Chimney* (given V Diff), there is nothing equivalent to a *Giant's Crawl*, maintaining its quality from the foot of the crag to the top at a grade that fits comfortably in this book.

Fortunately for the scrambler there is one celebrated chink in Scafell's armour: *Broad Stand*, pioneered by the Romantic poet Samuel Taylor Coleridge, provides a short, but tricky, stair from Mickledore at the head of Wasdale to the summit plateau. You will not quite be following in Coleridge's footsteps, as he happened upon the *Stand's* awkward shelves in descent and was lucky to avoid injury (see page 149). In ascent it becomes a more reasonable proposition – provided the rock is dry!

Broad Stand is preceded in this day out from Wasdale by an entertaining climb up *Crenation Ridge* (aka 'Cremation Ridge') on Pikes Crag, on the opposite side of Mickledore from Scafell Crag. The ridge is graded Diff but there is no strict line. Its inclusion cuts out some of the flog up from Hollow Stones to Mickledore and, unlike its brooding neighbour, Pikes Crag catches plenty of sunshine.

Route 18 also features a climb on Pikes Crag: *Grooved Arête* (V Diff), which lies a short distance left of *Crenation Ridge*. There is scope for mix and match. *Crenation Ridge* could be climbed as an easier alternative to *Grooved Arête* in Route 18; however including the *Arête* with *Broad Stand* is not so attractive. *Grooved Arête* is tough for the grade and requires a full rack; you might not want to be weighed down with a heavy pack all the way over Scafell.

Between Wasdale Head and Hollow Stones you will be on one of the busiest paths in the Lake District, part of the shortest route to England's highest mountain. At Hollow Stones the path to Scafell Pike bears off left and you continue ahead towards either Pikes Crag or direct to Mickledore and *Broad Stand*.

The day ends with a long stroll down Green How, the broad western shoulder of Scafell, as grassy as its name suggests and a great place from which to watch the sun dipping towards the Irish Sea.

BROAD STAND & SCAFELL

DISTANCE: 12km **TOTAL ASCENT:** *c.*1,000m **START:** Wasdale Head GR: NY 187085 or NY 182075 **TIME:** 8hrs **CLIMBING:** *Crenation Ridge c.*100m, Diff **SCRAMBLING:** *Broad Stand c.*50m, Grade 3+ **MAP:** OS Explorer OL6: The English Lakes South-western area, 1:25000 **REFRESHMENTS:** Wasdale Head Inn, Wasdale Head (T: 019467 26229)

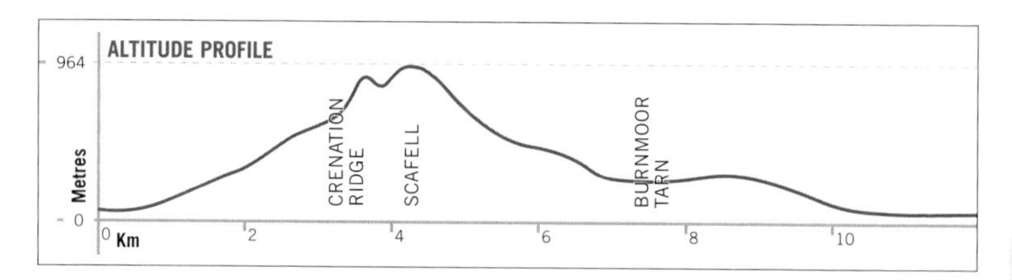

The Route
Broad Stand & Scafell

Start

Wasdale Head. Park either on the green at **GR: NY 187085**, about 400m before the Inn; or in the National Trust car park at **GR: NY 182075** near the head of Wast Water.

S **From the green:** walk south on the road for 200m, take a footpath south-east across meadows and over Lingmell Beck to a sheepfold, then bear south on the rising path that rounds the headland to join the Lingmell Gill path. **Or, from the car park at the head of Wast Water:** follow the track south-east over the bridge and bear left on a path beside the stream of Lingmell Gill. (Not to be confused with Lingmell *Beck*.) After bypassing the FRCC hut at Brackenclose, the path crosses to the north bank of Lingmell Gill.

2 The paths join and in *c.*500m ford Lingmell Gill. A well-engineered path now rises steadily for *c.*1km to the sloping bowl of Hollow Stones, distinguished by several very large boulders.

3 Hollow Stones. Scafell Crag looms above on the south side while the buttresses of Pikes Crag stand out directly ahead (south-east). The col of Mickledore lies between the two crags. The busy path to Scafell Pike bears off left here (roughly north-east) while we continue south-east towards Mickledore.

ROUTE CONTINUES OVERLEAF

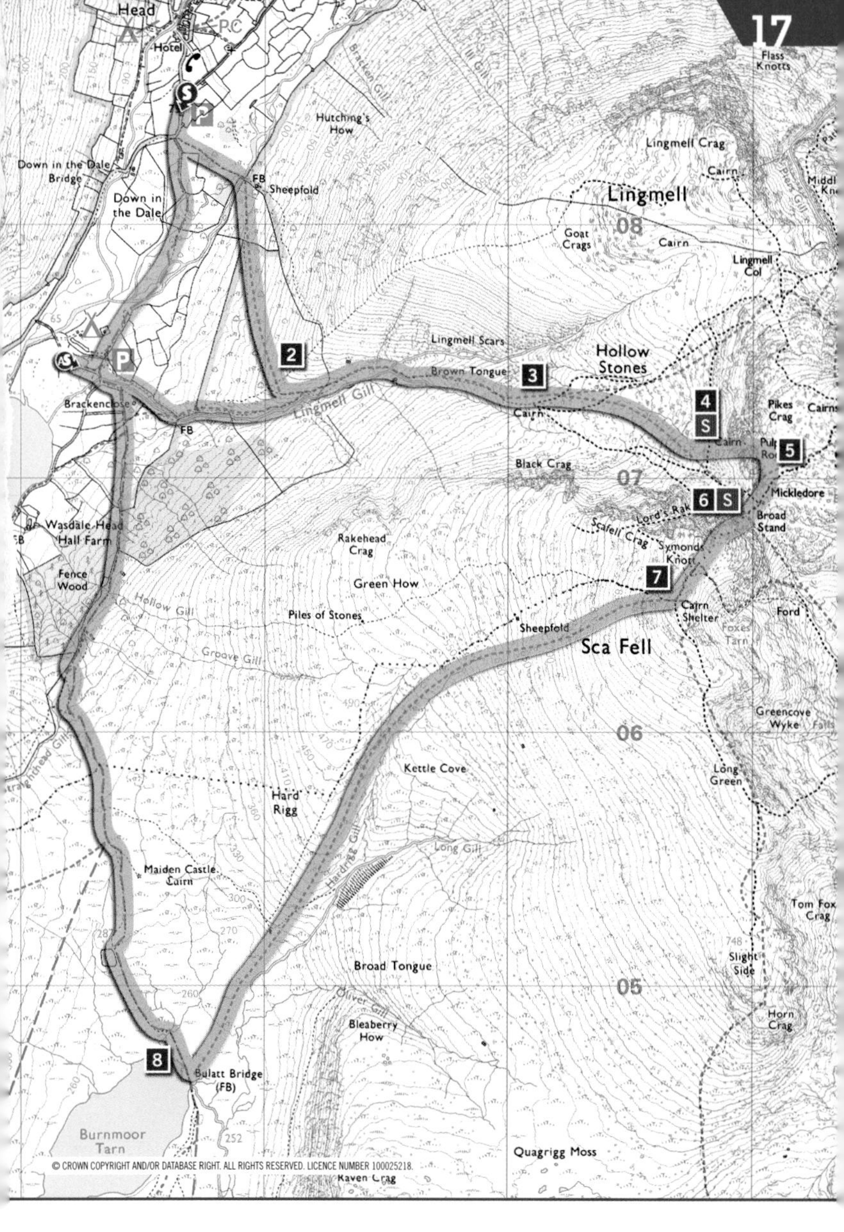
Wasdale Head
Row Head
PC
Hotel
Hutching's How
Bracken Gill
Down in the Dale Bridge
Down in the Dale
FB
Sheepfold
Lingmell Crag
Flass Knotts
Cairn
Lingmell
08
Goat Crags
Cairn
Lingmell Col
Lingmell Scars
Hollow Stones
Brown Tongue
Lingmell Gill
Brackenclose
FB
Cairn
Pikes Crag
Cairns
Black Crag
07
Mickledore
Broad Stand
Lord's Rake
Scafell Crag
Symonds Knott
Wasdale Head Hall Farm
Rakehead Crag
Fence Wood
Green How
Hollow Gill
Piles of Stones
Sheepfold
Cairn Shelter
Ford
Foxes Tarn
Sca Fell
Groove Gill
Greencove Wyke
Falls
06
Kettle Cove
Hard Rigg
Long Green
Long Gill
Hardrigg Gill
Maiden Castle Cairn
Tom Fox Crag
Broad Tongue
Slight Side
05
Oliver Gill
Bleaberry How
Horn Crag
Bulatt Bridge (FB)
Burnmoor Tarn
Quagrigg Moss
Raven Crag

4 **S** ***Crenation Ridge* (100m, Diff, E Ivison & D.R. Greenop, 1961)**

The ridge rises from the foot of a scree-filled gully that bounds the right-hand side of the crag. It is most easily approached by continuing on the Mickledore path until almost level with the foot of the gully and then traversing left to it across scree and rough ground.

Though several variations are possible, *Crenation Ridge* basically follows the arête on the left-hand side of the gully. Start at the gully's narrowest point where scrapes of earlier passage lead to a short wall and then gain the crest. Ascend broken rock and ledges, with just one awkward crack to possibly slow progress. Take care not to dislodge rubble on to your second.

The climb finishes on Pulpit Rock, the highest point of the crag, separated from the main mountain by a notch that necessitates either careful down-climbing into the notch or, safer, a short abseil.

5 After descending from Pulpit Rock to the notch, traverse above the gully, southwards, and soon join the path that descends from Scafell Pike to arrive in just a few minutes at Mickledore. (From the notch it is only a 15-minute walk up to the summit of Scafell Pike, the highest mountain in England, if desired.)

Pulpit Rock, topping Pikes Crag. Looking west to the Irish Sea.

To notch and descent route
Pulpit Rock
Grooved Arête
(Route 18)
Crenation Ridge 4
(Starts in gully and
is mostly out of sight)

Pikes Crag.

6 **S** ***Broad Stand* (*c*.50m, Grade 3+, S.T. Coleridge in descent, 1802)**

Starts about 25m down the Eskdale (east) side of Mickledore and ascends steps, shelves and broken ground to the plateau of Scafell. Left of Broad Stand soar the great test piece routes on the East Buttress – look and dream.

Start at a slit in the rock known as 'Fat Man's Agony'. Squeeze through this and climb to a sloping platform backed by a short (3m) wall with a corner on its right. This is the crux of the route – indeed it is the only real difficulty – and has been the scene of many accidents, including fatalities. **Great care must be taken. If the rock is wet, *Broad Stand* is best avoided.** It is possible to place a nut or cam in a crack on the right, but this provides only limited protection as you move above it.

Ease up the short wall or go more robustly up the corner. It is frustratingly awkward and makes the route almost ungradeable. From the platform is at least a V Diff sequence, but what follows is an easy scramble up ledges and a shallow gully. A path soon develops, leading above Scafell's buttresses to the summit cairn.

7 Scafell (964m). From the cairn, walk westwards off the stony top and on to the grassy flank of the mountain. A line in the grass trends gradually from west to south-west, spongy at the head of Kettle Cove, and then follows the ridge of Hard Rigg before dropping steeply to boggy ground bordering Burnmoor Tarn. While more direct lines are possible, to avoid wet feet it is best to follow the path to the edge of the tarn at Bulatt Bridge.

On Pulpit Rock; Wast Water below.

Squeezing through 'Fat Man's Agony', *Broad Stand*.

8 From Bulatt Bridge a good track (bridleway) leads northwards across the moor and eventually down by woods to Brackenclose and the National Trust car park. The bridleway runs along the east side of the NT campsite, crosses Lingmell Beck and continues on to the green and Wasdale Head Inn (4km from the tarn).

Though Samuel Taylor Coleridge is credited as the pioneer of *Broad Stand* and thus, by poetic licence, with making the first rock climb for sheer recreation, the author of *The Ancient Mariner* made no such claim himself. He was simply looking for a way off Scafell in the course of a nine-day solo 'circumcursion' of the Lake District and, working on his personal code of 'where it is first *possible* to descend, there I go', set off down easy ledges. But the drops became bigger, until he found himself contemplating one 'twice my own height'.

'The Ledge at the bottom was exceedingly narrow, that if I dropt down upon it I must of necessity have fallen backwards and of course killed myself. My Limbs were all in a tremble – I lay on my back to rest myself, and was beginning according to my Custom to laugh at myself for a Madman, when the sight of the Crags above me on each side, and the impetuous Clouds just over them, posting so luridly and rapidly northward, overawed me.

'I lay in a state of almost prophetic Trance and Delight ... O God, I exclaimed aloud, how calm, how blessed am I now. I know not how to proceed, how to return; but I am calm and fearless and confident.' And then he noticed a 'Rent' in the rock – presumably today's 'Fat Man's Agony' – and slipped down 'between two walls without danger or difficulty'.

Great Gable and The Napes from Scafell Pike.

James Berwick on *Grooved Arête's* sensational top pitch.

18 Grooved Arête & Scafell Pike Circuit

9km V Diff

A splendid climb to the top of England

WASDALE HEAD – LINGMELL GILL – HOLLOW STONES – PIKES CRAG (*Grooved Arête,* V Diff) – SCAFELL PIKE – LINGMELL – WASDALE HEAD

The day

Grooved Arête on Pikes Crag ranks high amongst my favourite V Diffs in the Lake District – possibly top of the list. Partly it is the quality of the route itself – cracks, a couple of chimneys and delightful slabs combining in an almost continuously entertaining line. It is quite hard for V Diff, with a delicate traverse early on and an awkward crack at half height, both of which would be pushing Severe were they not so protectable.

But it is the location that really elevates *Grooved Arête*. Pikes Crag forms the western rampart of Scafell Pike and looks across the cwm above Hollow Stones to the imposing buttresses and gullies of Scafell Crag. *Grooved Arête* rises to the summit of Pulpit Rock, the highest eminence of Pikes Crag, all the while gifting the climber an infinite view westwards over Wast Water to the Irish Sea and a close up of any action on the test pieces of Scafell Crag.

It really is an ascent in the crucible of Lakeland rock climbing, and furthermore it lands you within a stone's throw of the highest point of England – Scafell Pike itself.

The approach to Pikes Crag is the same as for Route 17, although our climb here is of a different order of difficulty. While *Crenation Ridge* (Route 17) is barely a Diff, has easy escape options and requires only a light rack, *Grooved Arête* calls for a full set of nuts and selection of cams. Double ropes are also recommended, making it easier to link the traditional pitches.

The pack may be heavier but there is not so far to carry it. The summit of Scafell Pike is only about 100 metres higher than the top of Pulpit Rock and after that it is an easy stroll to Lingmell Col. It would be possible to continue down from here to Hollow Stones, but the short ascent to the cairn on Lingmell is amply repaid by the panorama of the Wasdale fells and the sobering drop at your feet, 300 metres or so into the dark abyss of Piers Gill.

On the map, this does not look like a long day, and if you're match fit and climbing efficiently, it need not be. However Scafell Pike is as tall as they come in these parts, and the temptation to linger and savour the passage of *Grooved Arête* or the view from Lingmell is considerable.

GROOVED ARÊTE & SCAFELL PIKE CIRCUIT

DISTANCE: 9km **TOTAL ASCENT:** *c.*950m **START:** Wasdale Head GR: NY 187085 or NY 182075 **TIME:** 7–8hrs **CLIMBING:** *Grooved Arête*, 120m, V Diff **SCRAMBLING:** None **MAP:** OS Explorer OL6: The English Lakes South-western area, 1:25000 **REFRESHMENTS:** Wasdale Head Inn, Wasdale Head (T: 019467 26229)

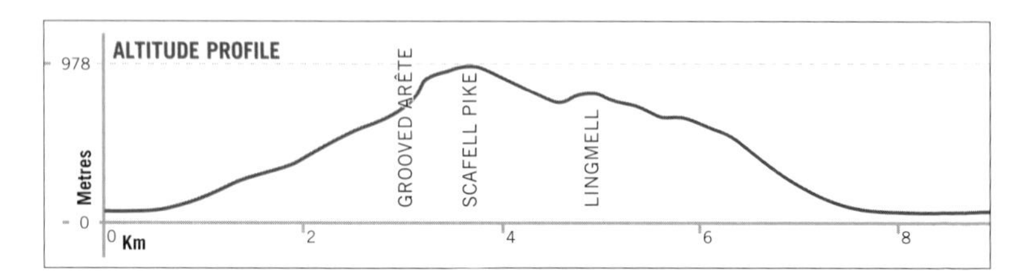

The Route
Grooved Arête & Scafell Pike Circuit

Start

As for **Route 17** at Wasdale Head. Park either on the green at **GR: NY 187085**, about 400m before the inn; or in the National Trust car park at **GR: NY 182075** near the head of Wast Water.

S **From the green:** walk south on the road for 200m, take a footpath south-east across meadows and over Lingmell Beck to a sheepfold, then bear south on the rising path that rounds the headland to join the Lingmell Gill path. **Or, from the car park at the head of Wast Water:** follow the track south-east over the bridge and bear left on a path beside the stream of Lingmell Gill. (Not to be confused with Lingmell *Beck*.) After bypassing the FRCC hut at Brackenclose, the path crosses to the north bank of Lingmell Gill.

2 The paths join and in *c.*500m ford Lingmell Gill. A well-engineered path now rises steadily for *c.*1km to the sloping bowl of Hollow Stones, distinguished by several very large boulders.

3 Hollow Stones. Scafell Crag looms above on the south side while the buttresses of Pikes Crag stand out directly ahead (south-east). The col of Mickledore lies between the two crags. The busy path to Scafell Pike bears off left here (roughly north-east) while we continue south-east towards Mickledore.

4 Stay on the Mickledore path until level with the foot of the crag then traverse leftwards across scree and broken ground.

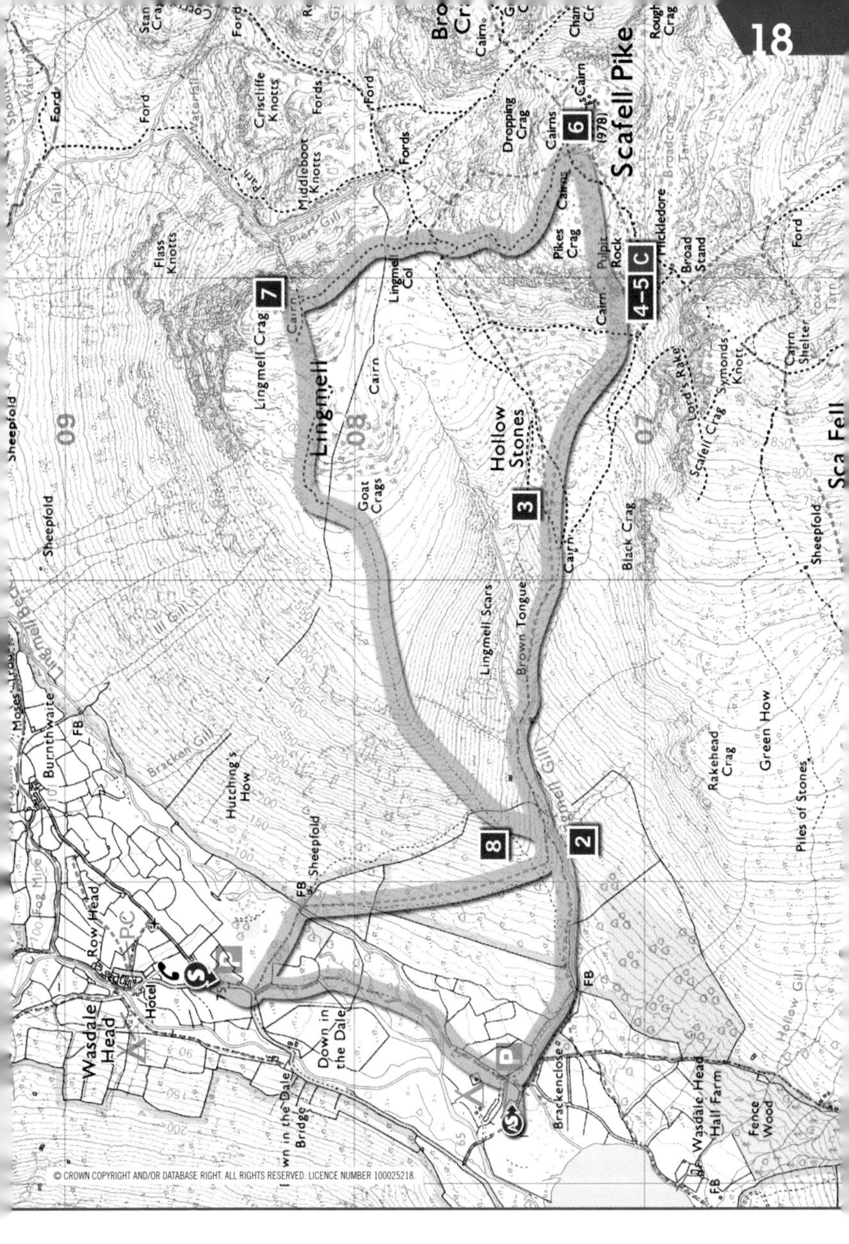
18
Scafell Pike
(978)
Lingmell
Lingmell Crag
Lingmell Col
Hollow Stones
Pikes Crag
Pulpit Rock
Mickledore
Broad Stand
Lord's Rake
Symonds Knott
Scafell Crag
Black Crag
Dropping Crag
Middleboot Knotts
Criscliffe Knotts
Piers Gill
Flass Knotts
Goat Crags
Lingmell Scars
Brown Tongue
Hutching's How
Bracken Gill
Ill Gill
Burnthwaite
Row Head
Wasdale Head
Hotel
Down in the Dale
Brackenclose
Wasdale Head Hall Farm
Fence Wood
Hollow Gill
Green How
Rakehead Crag
Piles of Stones
Sca Fell
Sheepfold
Cairn
Cairns
FB
1
2
3
4–5
6
7
8
C
09
08
07
© CROWN COPYRIGHT AND/OR DATABASE RIGHT. ALL RIGHTS RESERVED. LICENCE NUMBER 100025218.

5 **C** ***Grooved Arête* (120m, V Diff, C.F. Holland & G.R. Speaker, 1924).**

The route begins at the foot of the arête that bounds the right side of the main face (well left of *Crenation Ridge*), in a small bay below an overhang. Scramble up grassy ledges to the bay.

P1 30m: Scramble rightwards to gain a grassy groove ascending leftwards to a steep crack rising to the left edge of the overhang. Climb the crack for *c*.8m then make a delicate traverse left on small holds to pull over onto the arête. Move easily up the arête to a grass ledge and belay in the chimney beyond.

This pitch could be split into two pitches, belaying below the crack. This is probably desirable if climbing on a single rope, but if using double ropes (better on this route) there is no need.

P2 25m: Climb the chimney and the broken groove above. Move rightwards up grass ledges to belay at the foot of a square-cut corner.

P3 20m: The crack at the back of the corner is challenging for the first few moves but yields to give a satisfying pitch, finishing with a traverse right to a prominent block perched at the edge.

P4 30m: Climb the slab above, trending leftwards at first then back right, close to the arête, and move up blocks and ledges to a possible belay on the edge. Step left on to a slabby ramp and follow this to the foot of a chimney capped by a huge chockstone. (The chockstone is clearly visible on the approach to the crag.) Climb the chimney left of the chockstone and belay on its top.

P5 15m: Follow a ledge leftwards and down and pull round to regain the slabby front of the arête. Savour the final moves of the route, ascending the slab on small edges until a broken crack deposits you on the summit of Pulpit Rock.

Pulpit Rock is the highest point of the crag, separated from the main mountain by a notch reached by either careful down-climbing or, safer, a short abseil. From the notch it is only a 15-minute walk east up the stony brow of Scafell Pike to the summit plinth.

ROUTE CONTINUES OVERLEAF

Descent route off far side
of Pulpit Rock
Pulpit
Rock
5 Grooved Arête
Crenation Ridge
(Route 17)
Pikes Crag.

Julian Cooper on the airy top pitch of *Grooved Arête*.

6 Scafell Pike (978m). Walk north-west from the summit. Lingmell soon comes into view. A cairned path leads north down to Lingmell Col. **Do not** bear off left on the major path that leads down to Hollow Stones, unless omitting Lingmell. Instead continue ahead (north-north-west) up the fell to the blocky summit.

7 Lingmell (807m). After marvelling at the drop to Piers Gill and the view of the Wasdale fells, descend west at first, then trending south-west on the broad ridge looking towards Wast Water. The latter part of the descent to rejoin the outward route above the north bank of Lingmell Gill is steep and knee-jarring.

8 Depending on where you are parked, either continue down the gill path to Brackenclose and the NT car park or take the path descending the fellside north-north-west at first and on, over Lingmell Beck, to the green.

Pulpit Rock and Wast Water.

The 'Grand Stone': the north face of Pillar Rock above Ennerdale.

19 **Pillar Rock**

12km Hard V Diff

Two classics on the 'Grand Stone'

WASDALE HEAD – MOSEDALE – BLACK SAIL PASS – HIGH LEVEL ROUTE – PILLAR ROCK (*New West Climb* and *Slab and Notch*, both Hard V Diff) **– PILLAR – BLACK SAIL PASS – WASDALE HEAD**

The day

In his historical notes to the 1935 FRCC guide to Pillar Rock, editor H.M. Kelly recalled a gathering of scores of climbers and onlookers in April 1926 for the centenary of the Rock's first ascent. In front of Kelly was an elderly farmer and his wife gazing up at the 'great sweep' of the crag. 'Ay, it's a Grand Stone,' the farmer said simply. And in *New West Climb* and *Slab and Notch* are two routes that weave up and over this monumental 'stone' at a grade that seems, on initial, eye-widening sight, to be improbable.

While Coleridge is sometimes credited as having made 'the first rock climb' with his 1802 descent of *Broad Stand*, it was inadvertent; he was simply looking for a quick way off Scafell. Not so John Atkinson, the Ennerdale shepherd who climbed to the top of Pillar Rock on 9 July 1826 – some forty years before W.P. Haskett-Smith's landmark ascent of Napes Needle.

The Rock – or Pillar Stone as it was known – rears on a shoulder of Pillar fell and is accessible only by climbing steep rock. Atkinson is unlikely to have been looking for sheep there, so it is assumed he made the ascent for the challenge or sheer fun of it.

The Rock became a magnet for the pioneers of rock climbing in England. Many were professional men from the cities, sallying forth from Wasdale Head, but the first ascent party on *New West* included enterprising locals George and Ashley Abraham from Keswick.

It is hard to imagine 'scores' of climbers gathering at Pillar Rock today. High crags requiring a long walk-in went out of fashion decades ago. And few come higher and wilder than Pillar. A visit to the Rock takes commitment and the best part of a week of dry weather. But what a reward: one of the best V Diffs in England, moments of sensational, yet well-protected exposure and absorbing pitches of down-climbing on *Slab and Notch* to complete your crossing of the Grand Stone.

The route described here follows in the footsteps of the pioneers from their headquarters at Wasdale Head and traverses the gullies and broken crags on the northern flank of the Pillar massif – the High Level Route – to reach the Rock. An alternative is the approach up Ennerdale from the car park by Ennerdale Water. On foot this is pretty tedious, taking some three hours, but it can be made bearable by using bikes to GR: NY 169131 from where a rough path ascends south-west to below the Rock. The ride back is a treat.

PILLAR ROCK

DISTANCE: 12km **TOTAL ASCENT:** *c.*1,050m **START:** Green near Wasdale Head GR: NY 187085 **TIME:** 9hrs
CLIMBING: *New West Climb*, 85m, Hard V Diff; *Slab and Notch*, in descent -50m, Mod **SCRAMBLING:** None
MAPS: OS Explorers OL4 & OL6: The English Lakes North-western and South-western areas, 1:25000
(Almost all of route on OL4) **REFRESHMENTS:** Wasdale Head Inn, Wasdale Head (T: 019467 26229)

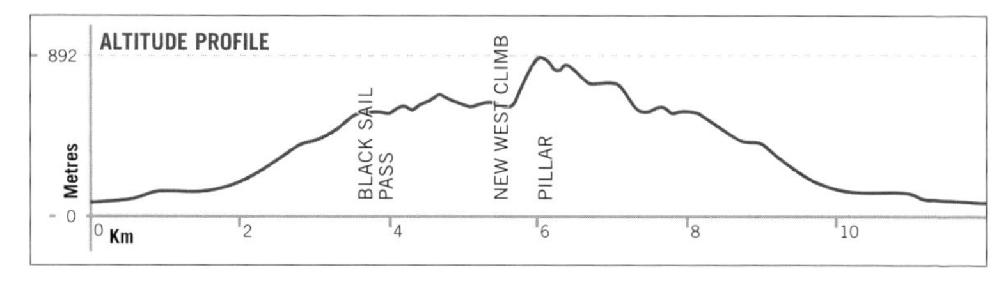

The Route **Pillar Rock**

Start

Wasdale Head, park on the green at **GR: NY 187085.**

S From the green, follow the lane north to the Wasdale Head Inn. Turn left at the Barn Door shop (weather forecast posted here), pass the public bar of the inn and turn right on the path on the east bank of the stream. **Do not** cross the stream. Continue generally north on the track up Mosedale.

2 At a large cairn 2km from the start, keep to the main path bearing uphill. (A minor path bears off left to continue up the floor of Mosedale.) Pass through the gate/stile and ford Gatherstone Beck. The path ascends steadily north-east then east to Black Sail Pass.

3 Black Sail Pass (*c.*400m). At the col turn left and follow the ridge path ascending north-west. Soon the path skirts to the left of the grassy top of Looking Stead. A slight diversion to the top of Looking Stead is rewarded with a splendid view of Ennerdale and of the craggy escarpment traversed by the High Level Route.

4 Very soon after descending from Looking Stead and rejoining the main path a cairn is reached marking the start of the High Level Route. Break right from the main path onto the Ennerdale face of the massif. A short, skittery descent is followed by an equally short scramble up to a point where the path splits. Both lines traverse the hillside and soon rejoin. I prefer the higher option.

ROUTE CONTINUES OVERLEAF

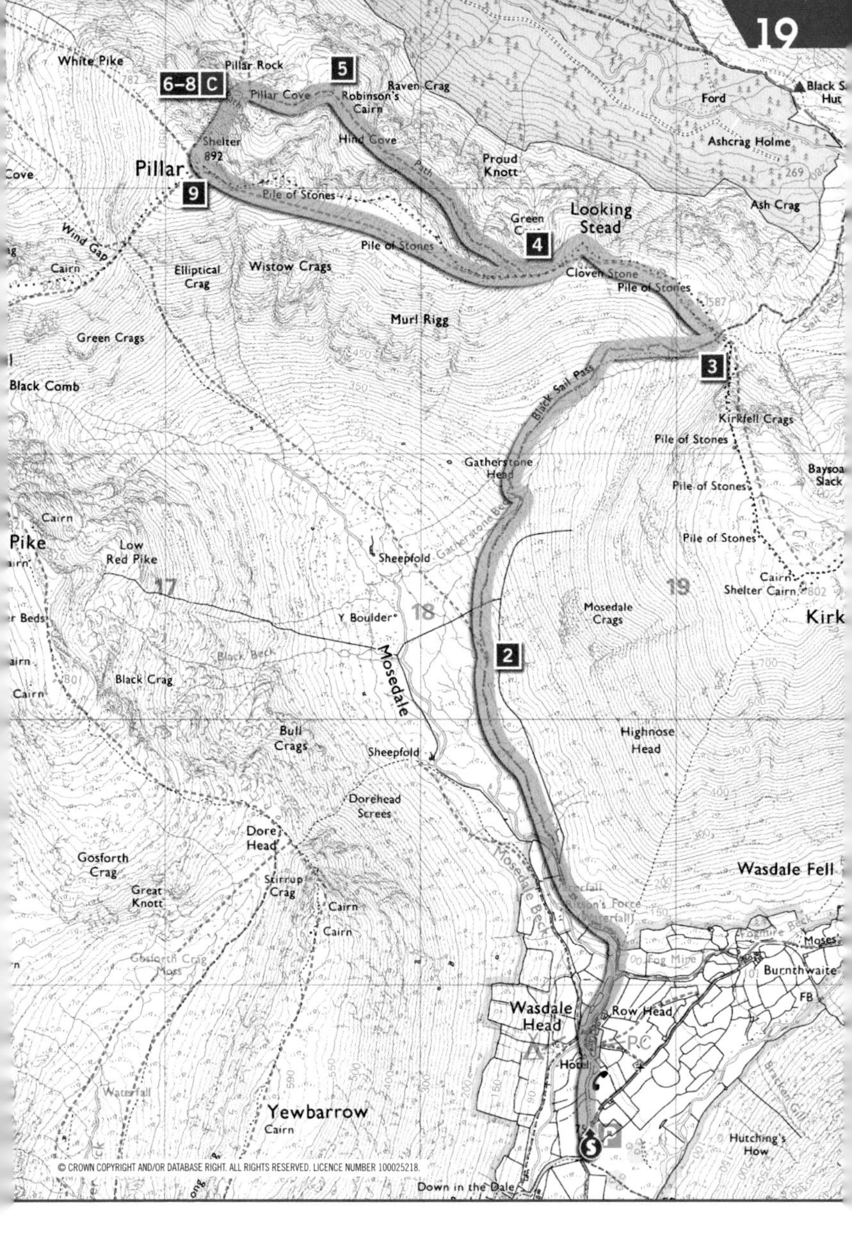
White Pike
Pillar Rock
6–8
C
5
Pillar Cove
Robinson's Cairn
Raven Crag
Hind Cove
Shelter 892
Pillar
9
Pile of Stones
Proud Knott
Looking Stead
Green Cove
4
Pile of Stones
Wind Gap
Cairn
Elliptical Crag
Wistow Crags
Cloven Stone
Pile of Stones
Murl Rigg
Green Crags
3
Black Sail Pass
Black Comb
Kirkfell Crags
Pile of Stones
Gatherstone Head
Pile of Stones
Gatherstone Beck
Cairn
Low Red Pike
Sheepfold
Pile of Stones
Cairn
Shelter Cairn
Y Boulder
Mosedale Crags
Kirk
Black Beck
Mosedale
2
Black Crag
Cairn
Bull Crags
Highnose Head
Sheepfold
Dorehead Screes
Dore Head
Gosforth Crag
Mosedale Beck
Wasdale Fell
Stirrup Crag
Great Knott
Cairn
Cairn
Gosforth Crag Moss
Fog Mire
Burnthwaite
Wasdale Head
Row Head
FB
Hotel
Waterfall
Yewbarrow
Cairn
Hutching's How
Black Sail Hut
Ford
Ashcrag Holme
Ash Crag
Down in the Dale

5 The HLR contours north-west past Robinson's Cairn and into a bouldery cove with the east face of Pillar Rock ahead. A worn way zigzags up scree then breaks right up a broad rake known as the Shamrock Traverse to a col between the main mountain and the craggy upthrust of Pisgah. Pillar Rock itself is separated from Pisgah by the sharp declivity of the Jordan Gap. (The geography of this whole area can be studied to advantage from Robinson's Cairn.)

6 The col sits directly above Western Gully. This is a good place to leave rucksacks so the climbing can be enjoyed unencumbered. Descend the scree of Western Gully, taking care not to cascade rocks onto others. The gully curves round beneath the west face of the Rock. The first prominent feature is the slit of the West Jordan Gully, leading up to the eponymous Gap. Pass a large block in the bed of Western Gully.

7 **C** ***New West Climb* (85m, Hard V Diff, G.D. Abraham, A.P. Abraham, C.W. Barton, J.H. Wigner, 1901)**

Start *c.*5m below the prominent block and just above a second block which lies embedded deep in the scree.

P1 **20m:** Climb a left-slanting groove above the embedded rock and onto a short rib. Then move easily rightwards to a large ledge.

P2 **10m:** Climb a shallow chimney to a small platform, then traverse left 4m to a good belay.

P3 **15m:** A groove is followed to ledges and a tricky traverse left to the foot of a steep chimney.

P4 **20m:** A traditional awkward chimney. Struggle up to the blocking chockstone. Turn this on the right and traverse rightwards, somewhat delicately around a rib, and up over blocks to a fine belay.

P5 **20m:** Climb the slab above by a crack to a ledge, then continue pleasantly up slabs on the left to finish almost at the cairn on top of High Man – the highest point of Pillar Rock.

ROUTE CONTINUES OVERLEAF

Pillar Rock – West Face of High Man.

8 **C** ***Slab and Notch*** **(in descent, -50m, Mod, 1863)**

In descent. Rope advisable.

Some 10m north of the cairn is the top of the Great Chimney that splits the east face of the Rock. Descend the chimney for several metres, then move left (facing in) to a broken slab and descend this and a short nose to the Notch. A steep corner lies on its far side. Down-climb the corner and cross the Slab to East Jordan Gully.

See topo. From the foot of the East Jordan Gully, chose between a): contouring below the east face of Pisgah to join the path up to the col at **Point 5** above the Western Gully; or b): scrambling up East Jordan Gully and at its top traversing leftwards to the west rib of Pisgah and following this to the top. Known as the *Pisgah West Traverse*, this 10m climb is graded only Moderate but has unsettling exposure. From the top it is a short scramble down to the col.

Pillar Rock – east face of Pisgah and High Man.

(The east face of Pisgah sports a pair of chimney climbs on clean rock, both graded Moderate, which give a few minutes of fun. *See topo.*)

From the col a rough path, scrambly in parts, ascends south-west to Pillar mountain. A cairn stands on the lip of the plateau with the main summit barely a minute's walk south.

9 Pillar (892m). The summit is marked by a survey column and windbreak cairns. For the return, a well-cairned path leads east-south-east from the summit, following a line of old iron fence posts and generally keeping close to the edge of the escarpment. This joins the outward route at **Point 4**. Continue down via Black Sail Pass and Mosedale.

Eric Parker (white top) solos the descent of *Slab and Notch*. In ascent this is the easiest route onto High Man.

Steeple, seen from above Mirk Cove, with Ennerdale below.
Steeple Buttress is the obvious sweep of rock from the summit into the cove.

20 Steeple Buttress & Yewbarrow Circuit

15.5km V Diff

A mountaineering day par excellence

OVERBECK BRIDGE BY WAST WATER – NETHER BECK – SCOAT FELL – MIRK COVE – *Steeple Buttress*, V Diff **– STEEPLE – RED PIKE – YEWBARROW – OVERBECK BRIDGE**

The day

This long day on the high fells of the west is one of my favourites. The remote setting of the east face climb (yet most of it on clean rock), the fact that it finishes hard by Steeple's summit cairn, and then the long drift out over Red Pike and Yewbarrow, drinking in a panorama from Gable and the Scafells to the Irish Sea … It really is the epitome of Lakeland mountaineering.

Steeple Buttress is accorded two stars in the FRCC guide, yet it is climbed, at most, infrequently. Hardly surprising – any climbing trip up Ennerdale demands time and energy, plus good fortune with the weather. Given the commitment, Pillar Rock, with its plethora of great routes, is the natural choice, rather than the lonely ramparts of Steeple.

Approached from Wasdale, however, *Steeple Buttress* becomes a more attractive proposition: the walk-in, though similar in time to that from Ennerdale (about 3 hours), is at a steadier gradient and much less arduous; and with the felltop return, including the traverse of Yewbarrow, the climb forms the zesty core of a constantly absorbing day.

After a short walk along Wast Water, the first couple of hours is spent following Nether Beck to the col between Haycock and Scoat Fell. Steeple comes into view almost at the highest point of the day's round – the misleadingly entitled (according to the OS map) 'Little' Scoat Fell at 841 metres. You'll already have walked over 'Great' Scoat Fell, but that is only 802 metres.

Broken cliffs and steep coves plunge towards Ennerdale, with Steeple dramatically set on a ridge connected to the main fell by a narrow, dipping neck. The buttress climb begins almost below your feet in Mirk Cove. As you descend – with care – into the head of the cove, you realise a treat is in store. A rib of coarse-textured rock leads continuously – or so it seems at first – from the foot of the cliffs to the top of Steeple, which from here appears more a wildly gothic pulpit than a shapely spire.

At 160 metres, few routes in the Lake District are this long, and even though there turns out to be a short grassy scramble in the middle, you will be well satisfied by the time you touch the summit cairn. You might even wonder whether the top section isn't somewhat undergraded at V Diff, particularly in such a committing location. Feel good about it as you head for the promenade over Yewbarrow.

STEEPLE BUTTRESS & YEWBARROW CIRCUIT

DISTANCE: 15.5km **TOTAL ASCENT:** 1,375m **START:** Overbeck Bridge GR: NY 168068 **TIME:** 9hrs **CLIMBING:** *Steeple Buttress* 160m, V Diff **SCRAMBLING:** None **MAP:** OS Explorers OL4 & OL6: The English Lakes North-western and South-western areas, 1:25000 **REFRESHMENTS:** Wasdale Head Inn, Wasdale Head (T: 019467 26229)

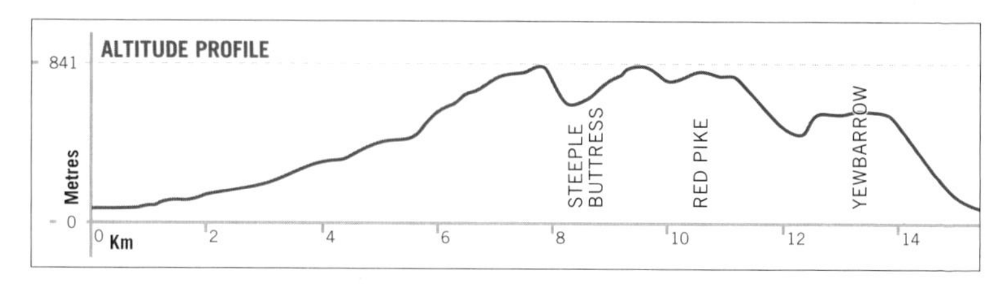

The Route
Steeple Buttress & Yewbarrow Circuit

Start

Overbeck Bridge, Wasdale. Car park on the east side of the bridge. **GR: NY 168068.**

S Turn right from the car park and walk west on the road by Wast Water for 700m to cross Netherbeck Bridge.

2 After a further 300m turn sharp right on a path leading up Nether Beck valley. (It is possible to short cut this corner after crossing the bridge, but it is boggy ground.) Continue steadily northwards up the valley.

3 About 4km up the valley, below Little Lad Crag, a faint path bears off rightward, crosses the beck near a prominent outcrop and climbs north-east towards Scoat Tarn. This offers a shorter, though often boggy, way to the head of Mirk Cove. We, however, continue northward for a further 1km to the col (*c.*710m) between Haycock and Scoat Fell – as this is the better, and certainly more aesthetic, route.

4 At the col turn right and follow the path on the south side of the wall up the fell. After 1km, cross the wall to a large cairn overlooking the narrow north-north-west ridge on which rises Steeple.

5 The cairn (*c.*835m) offers a good vantage point to view *Steeple Buttress*, the most continuous line of rock descending from the summit into Mirk Cove, and also your options for descending into the cove itself. The surest way is to continue east-north-east over Little Scoat Fell to the lowest point of the col above Mirk Cove then descend carefully and traverse to the foot of the east face. Scramble leftwards over easy-angled rock and grass to the blunt toe of the rib on the left side of face.

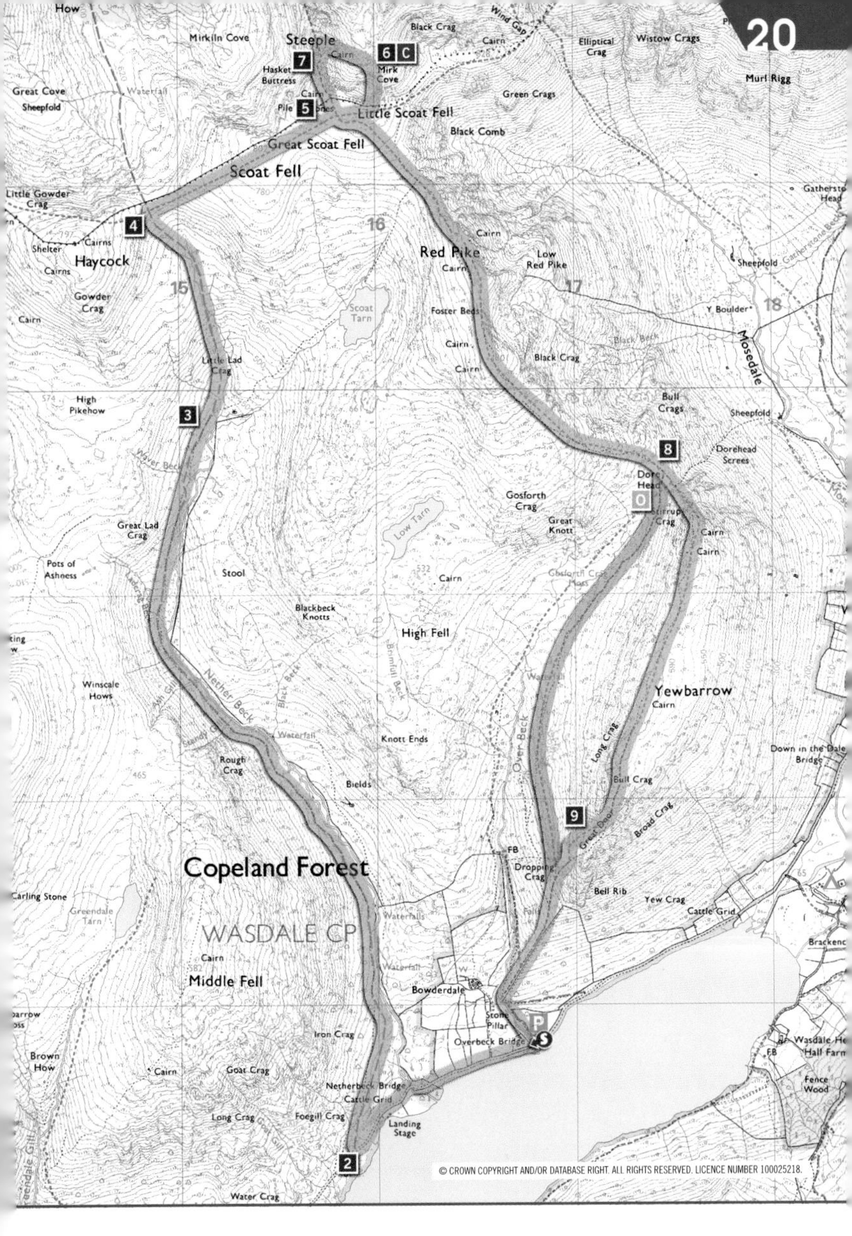
How
Mirkiln Cove
Steeple
Black Crag
Wind Gap
Cairn
Elliptical Crag
Wistow Crags
Murl Rigg
7
6
C
Hasket Buttress
Mirk Cove
Great Cove
Sheepfold
Waterfall
5
Pile
Little Scoat Fell
Green Crags
Black Comb
Great Scoat Fell
Scoat Fell
Little Gowder Crag
Gatherstone Head
4
16
Cairns
Shelter
Haycock
Red Pike
Low Red Pike
Sheepfold
Gatherstone Beck
15
Gowder Crag
Scoat Tarn
Foster Beds
17
Y Boulder
18
Black Beck
Mosedale
Black Crag
Little Lad Crag
High Pikehow
3
Bull Crags
Sheepfold
8
Dorehead Screes
Waver Beck
Dore Head
0
Gosforth Crag
Stirrup Crag
Great Knott
Great Lad Crag
Low Tarn
Pots of Ashness
Stool
Gosforth Crag Moss
Blackbeck Knotts
High Fell
Winscale Hows
Nether Beck
Black Beck
Bromfell Beck
Yewbarrow
Long Crag
Over Beck
Waterfall
Knott Ends
Rough Crag
Bull Crag
Bields
9
Broad Crag
Great Door
Copeland Forest
FB
Dropping Crag
Bell Rib
Yew Crag
Carling Stone
Greendale Tarn
Cattle Grid
Waterfalls
WASDALE CP
Brackenclose
Cairn
Waterfall
Middle Fell
Bowderdale
Stone Pillar
P
Down in the Dale Bridge
Overbeck Bridge
Wasdale Head Hall Farm
Iron Crag
Brown How
Cairn
Goat Crag
FB
Netherbeck Bridge
Cattle Grid
Fence Wood
Long Crag
Foegill Crag
Landing Stage
2
Greendale Gill
Water Crag

6 **C** ***Steeple Buttress* (160m, V Diff, D.A. Elliott, 1957)**

Start at the foot of the rib (*c*.680m). Frequent variations of the route are possible.

P1 **30m:** Ascend the rib to a grassy platform at a short (*c*.4m) wall with an obvious crack on its right side.

P2 **45m:** Ascend the wall either by the crack or, more easily, on its left edge to gain the crest of the rib. (The FRCC guide splits this pitch in two, belaying at a recess at around half height.) The climbing on the rib is delicate in places but the rock is reassuringly rough. Belay at a small ledge where a medium sized nut slots perfectly into a crack.

P3 **35m:** Scramble up rocks and grass near the right edge of the buttress, then traverse left to belay at the foot of a rib leading to the top.

P4 **25m:** Gain the rib by an awkward step up to its left side; continue steeply and belay at a large block.

P5 **25m:** Above loom two uninviting greasy chimneys. Ignore these and instead ascend a steep groove on the left, soon stepping up on its left side to superb holds, airily positioned, and a finish on easier rock leading almost to the summit cairn.

Steeple Buttress as seen from the back of Mirk Cove.

7 From the cairn at the top of Steeple (826m) traverse the notch to the felltop at **Point 5** and cross the wall to its south side. From here an obvious path leads south-east over Red Pike (826m) and down to Dore Head, 3km from Steeple.

8 Yewbarrow is now directly ahead; its 1.5km crest is gained by a path, almost a scramble in places, that zigzags up alongside Stirrup Crag.

O If time or energy is lacking for another ascent, Yewbarrow can be bypassed by either of two paths that descend from Dore Head directly to Overbeck Bridge; the drier skirts the west flank of Yewbarrow.

9 From the south end of Yewbarrow, a path (skittery in places) descends steeply by Dropping Crag and the fell nose to the car park at Overbeck Bridge.

Phil Blanshard on the lower rocks of *Steeple Buttress.*

Descending to Dore Head with Yewbarrow ahead.

Appendix

The following is a list of Tourist Information Centres, shops, cafes, pubs, websites and other contacts that might come in handy.

Tourist Information Centres

Cumbria Tourism .... www.golakes.co.uk
Official website of the Lake District National Park .... www.lakedistrict.gov.uk
Ambleside, Central Buildings, Market Cross
0844 225 0544 ... tic@thehubofambleside.com
Coniston, Ruskin Avenue 01539 441 533
mail@conistontic.org .... www.conistontic.org
Grasmere, Red Bank Road . 01539 435 245
Kendal, Made in Cumbria, Stramongate,
01539 735 891 .... info@kendaltic.com
Keswick, Market Square 01768 775 043
.... keswicktic@lakedistrict.gov.uk
.... www.lakedistrict.gov.uk
Penrith 01768 867 466
pen.tic@eden.gov.uk .... www.visiteden.co.uk
Seatoller, Borrowdale 01768 777 294
Ullswater, Beckside Car Park,
Glenridding 01768 482 414
.... ullswatertic@lakedistrict.gov.uk
.... www.lakedistrict.gov.uk
Windermere, Glebe Road 01539 488 005
.... BownessTIC@lakedistrict.gov.uk
.... www.lakedistrict.gov.uk

Food and Drink

(See individual routes for recommendations.)

Cafés

Shepherd's 'Caff', High Lodore Farm, Borrowdale
Wilf's, Staveley 01539 822 329
.... www.wilfs-cafe.co.uk
Bluebird Café, Coniston 01539 441 649
.... www.thebluebirdcafe.co.uk
The Old Sawmill Tearoom,
Mirehouse 01768 774 317
Chesters, Skelwith Bridge 01539 434 711
.... www.chestersbytheriver.co.uk
Fellbites, Glenridding 01768 482 781
.... www.fellbitescafe.co.uk
Rydal Hall Tea Room, Rydal ... 01539 432 050

Pubs

Golden Rule, Ambleside 01539 432 257
.... www.goldenrule-ambleside.co.uk
Old Dungeon Ghyll Hotel, Gt Langdale
01539 437 272 .... www.odg.co.uk
The Mill Inn, Mungrisdale 01768 779 632
.... www.the-millinn.co.uk
Travellers Rest, Glenridding ... 01768 482 298
The Wasdale Head Inn 01946 726 229
.... www.wasdale.com
Wainwrights' Inn, Chapel Stile
01539 438 088 .... www.langdale.co.uk

Accommodation

Youth Hostels

YHA Youth Hostels can be found in the following places. For more information please visit **www.yha.org.uk**

Ambleside 0845 371 9620
Borrowdale 0845 371 9624
Coniston (Coppermines) 0845 371 9630
Grasmere (Butharlyp Howe) ... 0845 371 9319
Helvellyn 0845 371 9742
Keswick 0845 371 9746
Langdale 01539 437 579
Skiddaw House 07747 174 293
Wasdale Hall 0845 371 9350
Windermere 0845 371 9352

Bunkhouses, B&Bs and Hotels

www.staylakedistrict.co.uk

For specific information, contact a Tourist Information Centre in the area in which you intend to stay.

Camping

Wasdale Head Campsite, Wasdale
01946 726 220 .... www.nationaltrust.org

Chapel House Farm Campsite, Borrowdale, ... 01768 777 256
.... www.chapelhousefarmcampsite.co.uk

Great Langdale, Langdale 01539 437 668
.... www.nationaltrust.org.uk

There are many, many more campsites in the Lake District – try www.coolcamping.co.uk or www.golakes.co.uk

Weather

www.metoffice.gov.uk www.mwis.org.uk

Outdoor Shops

There are innumerable climbing and outdoor shops in the Lake District.

Needle Sports, Keswick 01768 772 227
.... www.needlesports.com

George Fisher Ltd 01768 772 178
.... www.georgefisher.co.uk

planetFear, Keswick 01768 800 504
.... www.planetfear.com

The Epicentre, Ambleside 01539 528 528
.... www.theepicentre.co.uk

The Climbers Shop, Ambleside
01539 430 122 ...... www.climbers-shop.com

Cotswold Outdoor, Keswick, Grasmere and Ambleside .... www.cotswoldoutdoor.com

Stewart Cunningham, Ambleside
01539 432 636 .... www.srcunningham.co.uk

The Barn Door Shop, Wasdale Head
01946 726 384 ..... www.barndoorshop.co.uk

Freetime, Carlisle www.freetime1.co.uk

Nevisport, Kendal
01539 734 428 .... www.nevisport.com

Outdoor@Rheged, Rheged Centre
01768 860 046 .... www.rheged.com

Other Publications

Day Walks in the Lake District
Stephen Goodwin
Vertebrate Publishing, www.v-publishing.co.uk

Lake District Mountain Landscape
Alastair Lee
Vertebrate Publishing, www.v-publishing.co.uk

Walking the Literary Landscape
Ian Hamilton & Diane Roberts
Vertebrate Publishing, www.v-publishing.co.uk

Lake District Mountain Biking – Essential Trails
Chris Gore & Richard Staton
Vertebrate Publishing, www.v-publishing.co.uk

Great Britain Mountain Biking
Tom Fenton & Andy McCandlish
Vertebrate Publishing, www.v-publishing.co.uk

Scafell & Wasdale
Al Phizacklea & Ron Kenyon
FRCC, www.frcc.co.uk

Langdale
Max Biden
FRCC, www.frcc.co.uk

Lake District Rock
FRCC Guidebooks Committee
FRCC, www.frcc.co.uk

Borrowdale
Gary Baum & Al Hewison
FRCC, www.frcc.co.uk

Further reading

Scrambling and climbing for fun in the Lake District has a history stretching back more than a century and a half. In that time a veritable library of guidebooks has been produced. Each looks to its predecessors while hopefully trying to add new ideas and possibilities. Yet classic routes – say *Needle Ridge* on The Napes or the *Pinnacle Ridge* scramble on St Sunday Crag – have not achieved that status for nothing. They are great routes and it would be perverse to leave them out for fear of repetition.

The aim with *Lake District Climbs and Scrambles* has been to present just twenty day-long expeditions rather than detail the possibilities on particular crags. But if in the course of these adventures you are inspired to revisit an area for a more intense cragging or scrambling day there are several good guides available. Over many years of climbing and roaming these fells I have benefited from the wisdom of many authors, notably Bill O'Connor (*Fifty Best Scrambles in the Lake District*, David & Charles), Brian Evans (*Scrambles in the Lake District*, vols 1 & 2, Cicerone) and Jon Sparks and Judith Brown (*Scrambles & Easy Climbs in the Lake District*, Grey Stone Books). Above all though I am indebted to generations of authors and editors of the definitive Climbing Guides to the English Lake District published by the Fell and Rock Climbing Club (FRCC).

Pikes Crag, Wasdale, from Hollow Stones. Low winter sun is catching *Grooved Arête* which rises to Pulpit Rock, the highest point of the crag, on the right.